THEOPOETICS IN COLOR

THEOPOETICS IN COLOR

Embodied Approaches in Theological Discourse

Edited by

OLUWATOMISIN OLAYINKA OREDEIN
LAKISHA R. LOCKHART-RUSCH

WILLIAM B. EERDMANS PUBLISHING COMPANY
GRAND RAPIDS, MICHIGAN

Wm. B. Eerdmans Publishing Co.
4035 Park East Court SE, Grand Rapids, Michigan 49546
www.eerdmans.com

Book design by Lydia Hall

Printed in the United States of America

ISBN 978-0-8028-8018-5

Library of Congress Cataloging-in-Publication Data

A catalog record for this book is available from the Library of Congress.

*For those who can now
rejoice because you are finally
heard and known: we see
you and celebrate (with) you.
This book, dear loves, is our
collective rejoicing.*

we write from the body.

—Nayyirah Waheed, "melanin | bone and soil"

Contents

Contents

Foreword

CLÁUDIO CARVALHAES

The book you have in your hands is like a colorful garden filled with different plants, flowers, vegetations, and soils, involving complex multivalent generative relations and affections. Its colors show different landscapes and forms of living and thinking. Life in its fullness. This book comes to us from the hearts/bodies/minds/spirits of scholars of various places and wisdom. As each of them wrestle with their own ways of living poetically, these scholars wrote these texts with their bodies, the desires of their hearts, the organization of their minds, and the offering of their spirit. We could also say the same thing by shifting words around. For example: this book was written with their hearts, the desires of their bodies, the organization of their spirits, and the offering of their minds. While there is distinction and difference in each chapter, there is no self-compartmentalization in their art making.

The fullness of this book is shown in the full-ness of each author's full being. Everything is at stake here: emotions, objectivity, subjectivity, longings, deep concerns, anger, cries, losses, joys, proposals, challenges, elucidations, utterances, sensibilities, and so on, all marked by the different postures and conditions of their hearts/bodies/minds/spirits. Each of them is marked and carried out by the communities who made them. In each chapter, we can see how the authors were made by the way that they write, the forms of knowledge they perceive in the world, and the elders and companions who travel with them as deep references.

This book engages and fosters new understandings of theopoetics. The authors have different flows of interpretations and they offer more and also less conclusive understandings of what theopoetics might mean and how it can be done. The wonderful introduction written by Oluwatomisin Olayinka Oredein offers a great organizing structure as well as historical and theological (*un*)framework of what theopoetics means, where it begins, how it moves and exists.

Theopoetics is life in process, never linear, never self-enclosed, never necessarily expected, never ordained, and never oriented to a clear telos. Instead, theopoetics not only witnesses to but comes from life in all its fullness, giving voice to the orders and disturbances, speaking from healing and from where it hurts, trying to figure out justices and injustices, breakdowns and resurrections, setbacks and opportunities, losses and blessings, unexpected turns, being lost and being found, perhaps again and again. As for God, God is in all these processes, not removed from these various paths, but God goes also *unfigured* in these pathways and markers. God is born through the knowing, through the birthing of the writers in their theopoetic processes of creation. In theopoetics, God can be as clear as water but can also be as elusive as a mirror. God moves in so close even at a distance and reveals Godself in the unfolding of many presences throughout journeys unfinished. The theopoetics of this book offers a diverse breadth of Christian interpretations of life, which made me remember the words of Meister Eckhart: "I once had a dream. Even though I am a man, I dreamt I was pregnant. Pregnant with nothingness; and out of this nothingness God was born."

That nothingness of which Eckhart is speaking is not emptiness but rather a fullness filled with possibilities. And that is what we see in this book: from the many places of fullness these writers come from, God is born in different ways. However, this birthing is never done alone but it is fundamentally communal. The community is the place of its birth, the place one belongs, leaves, and carries within oneself and which shapes theopoetics and these theopoets profoundly. That is why we can say that this book includes both metaphysical and ontological claims.

As I read this book, I was also reminded of Aristotle's form of autopoiesis and Donna Haraway's notion of sympoiesis. Theopoetics is more a work of sympoiesis than autopoiesis. Haraway defines the autopoietic as "self-forming, boundary maintaining, contingent, dynamic, and stable under some conditions but not others" and quotes M. Beth Dempster in defining sympoiesis as "collectively-producing systems."[1]

Theopoetics must follow biology and chemistry in thinking about life as sympoiesis. For life is never an event of a cell or an individual alone. Rather,

---

1. Donna J. Haraway, *Staying with the Trouble: Making Kin in the Chthulucene* (Durham, NC: Duke University Press, 2016), 33.

life is always collective, flexible, reoriented by other presences, and able to adapt. If in autopoiesis an organism has the illusion of producing itself like capitalism wants us to think, in sympoiesis, we are constantly engaging with the environments, producing other forms of composition in order to continue to exist. Because all systems are systems in relation to one another, there is no autonomy in that matter since the first process of life is indeed a symbiotic relationship. Thus, the autonomy of people should not be regarded as an individual task but rather a search for life in fullness, liberated, in complex correlations of belongings and mutuality that keep us alive.

In that sense the shape, format, and process of this book is fundamentally *sympoietic*. It was done with care and various forms of relations between the writers and the editors. The beautiful concluding conversation between Lakisha R. Lockhart-Rusch and Oluwatomisin Olayinka Oredein is fundamental in showing us a bit of the complexities of the methodology and the forms of relational and mutual care in the making of this book.

In the desert of theological ideas, this book is a seed bank, carrying seeds of life, liberation, and transformation. Come and travel in the fields of God, of the Gods. Get some of these seeds and take them home. Plant there and see how, in the correlations of your own soil, you can create new seeds of liberation and transformation.

Surely this book is the most important text on theopoetics in the English language. To these potent, precious, powerful writers and the editors we offer our deepest gratitude.

Introduction

Why Theopoetics, Why in Color?

OLUWATOMISIN OLAYINKA OREDEIN

In the spring of 2018, I taught an immersive course at a seminary on theopoetics called Embodied Theology: Race, Gender, and Performance in Popular Art. All of my students were Black. The course's initial title was Theopoetics but since my faculty colleagues could not pin down what *theopoetics* meant, I changed the name to Embodied Theology. It was the best way to move the course through the approval process.

As I had designed it, the course was intentionally focused on Black identity and Black modes of art in light of the question of theopoetics. But in order to have a discussion, we had to start at the beginning: What is theopoetics?

To get some answers to this question, we read Rubem Alves during the first week of class. The students felt lost, in a generative way. They did not know what to do with his liberated style of writing and indiscriminate engagements with difficult concepts. His explorations, however, felt close to who they were.

During the second week, the class read about process theology from experts Jay McDaniel and Donna Bowman. Again, they felt lost, but this time in a confused way. They were unsure of what the circuitous language and ideas offered had to do with theology known and done in bodies.

The lesson in starting the course this way was simple: we know God differently through our bodies. Thus, how we talk about the beginnings of anything—including the discourse of theopoetics—matters.

Oluwatomisin Olayinka Oredein

Two Stories from Genesis

What is most promising about beginnings is how they can be told from multiple angles. Within the Christian scriptural tradition, the creation accounts found in Genesis 1 and Genesis 2 are both pieced together to form one story, but they are also recognized as whole accounts within themselves.

With these two truths in hand, readers are edged toward what can be understood as the "truest" constructed version of what creation's beginnings might have been. Even within this pieced-together narrative, the strength of the individual stories stands in its own right. Both accounts grant a foundational picture by favoring a certain angle in telling the story.

The systematic format birthed from the Priestly sources of the fifth and sixth centuries BCE renders Genesis 1 a story of meticulous sequence and order. We receive a Creator-focused creation account, the ordering of the universe being that story's most prominent feature.[1]

The more narrative version from the Yahwist tradition of the ninth and tenth centuries BCE rings just as true! Genesis 2 gives us a human-focused account. We are able to imagine God's molding of humanity from the earth as illustrative of creation's relationship with itself. The material nature of creation—its tangibility, its dustiness—is the star of this particular account and storyline.[2]

While I do not argue that theopoetics has complete coherence with these narrative strands, I do find it helpful to frame our discourse on theopoetics through such narratives. The notion of theopoetics having two genesis stories helps us understand what it is and where it has come from. One theopoetic story is from a primarily White, philosophical perspective. The second theopoetic story is from non-White, minoritized voices who use their own experiences and techniques to do theopoetics in ways that makes sense to who they are.

---

1. See Catherine Keller, *The Face of the Deep: A Theology of Becoming* (New York: Routledge, 2003). I dare not brave the theoretical and theological webwork that Catherine Keller performs around distinguishing the difference between "beginnings" and "origins" in her chapter "Bottomless Surface: When Beginning" (see chapter 9 in *Face of the Deep*). The main takeaway relevant to this work is her point of the divine sanctioning of origin as genesis whereas beginnings can start within an origin. Origins, according to Keller, precede beginnings.

2. See Benjamin Valentine, *In Our Own Voices: Latino/a Renditions of Theology* (Maryknoll, NY: Orbis Books, 2010), 22; William C. Placher, ed., *Essentials of Christian Theology* (Louisville: Westminster John Knox, 2003), 94.

I typically call the first account "WASP Theopoetics," but academia has more candidly deemed it "theopoetics." The second does not have as deep a reputation as some of the initial voices of the theopoetics movement, but I and many marginalized persons have known it to have the same name as the first, "theopoetics."

For naming purposes and clarity within this introduction, the first narrative will concern "Traditional Theopoetics" and the latter, "Theopoetics in Color." The first has reactive origins in primarily White philosophical thought and liberal theology. Its thrust is relevance. The second has responsive origins in the cultural cues and theological ideologies of minority communities and their respective cultures. Its thrust is liberation.

TRADITIONAL THEOPOETICS

I believe that to know what theopoetics is, we need to look no further than introductions.[3] Literally.

The introductions of seminal theopoetics texts reveal the exclusive beginnings and uses of Traditional Theopoetics.

L. Callid Keefe-Perry's *Way to Water: A Theopoetics Primer* offers "a genealogy and history of a path called theopoetics"[4]—the first of its kind. He notes that the first published use of the term "theopoetics" was introduced to the world by Stanley Hopper at the 1971 American Academy of Religion meeting. Hopper's student David Miller would further flesh out the definition, characterizing theopoetics as a sort of theological meaning-making.[5] Theopoetics as an emerging discourse came to the fore in response to the questions of Christian theology's efficacy in that particular historical moment. While Hopper's task in employing theopoetics yielded a theologically thoughtful idea and direction, a conceptual limit was already present within it. Who had access to this latest theological direction? Who could contribute to its formation? It

---

3. I am fully aware that through this very introduction I have to do some "historical grounding" that centers White voices, a practice I name as problematic. This tension, however, serves a purpose. It illumines how few racial and ethnic minoritized scholars have historically been considered as part of this burgeoning conversation. Alas, to frame the dire problem of underrepresentation within theopoetic discourse I must name where we minorities are not present and have not been present across time.

4. L. Callid Keefe-Perry, introduction to *Way to Water: A Theopoetics Primer* (Eugene, OR: Cascade, 2014), 1.

5. Keefe-Perry, introduction, 2–3.

seemed that theopoetics' theological beginnings were revealed in a particular privileged academic company—White and male.

One man made famous for using theopoetic language soon after Hopper, Amos Wilder, understood theopoetics as breaking away from religious reflection addicted "to the discursive, the rationalistic, and the prosaic." In his book *Theopoetics*, he calls for a blossoming of theological imagination in America. The "Christian imagination must go halfway to meet the new dreams, mystiques, and the mythologies that are gestating in our time," he urged.[6] Like Hopper, Wilder was caught in the theological crisis happening within theological liberalism that would span well over a century. His response was to flesh out the discourse in the ways he knew how.

Gary Dorrien, a social ethicist and theologian familiar with theological liberalism's trajectory, frames liberalism in American theology as an ecumenical project centering a modern reformed take on Protestant Christian teaching.[7] It was a response to the question of Christian theology's lack of dynamism and imagination. A liberal approach to theology primarily seeks an epistemological flexibility away from the rigid, ancient standards of how theology was typically done at the time. This shift was needed in order for Christian theology to remain a significant force in the world—in thought life and in practice.

---

6. Amos Wilder, "Theology and Theopoetic," in *Theopoetic: Theology and the Religious Imagination* (Lima, OH: Academic Renewal, 2001), 1. The original edition was published in 1976 by Fortress Press.

7. Gary Dorrien, "Modernisms in Theology: Interpreting American Liberal Theology, 1805–1950," *American Journal of Theology & Philosophy* 23, no. 3 (September 2002): 200–220, especially 203, 205–6. Dorrien's full definition is helpful here to understand its layers. He writes,

> I define liberal theology primarily by its original character as a mediating Christian movement. Liberal Christian theology is a tradition that derives from the late eighteenth- and early nineteenth-century Protestant attempt to reconceptualize the meaning of traditional Christian teaching in the light of modern knowledge and modern ethical values. It is reformist in spirit and substance, not revolutionary. Fundamentally it is the idea of a genuine Christianity not based upon external authority. Liberal theology seeks to reinterpret the symbols of traditional Christianity in a way that creates a progressive religious alternative to secular unbelief and to theologies based on external authority. Specifically, it is defined by its acceptance of modern knowledge, especially historical criticism and modern science; its commitment to the authority of individual reason and experience; its conception of Christianity as an ethical way of life; its favoring of moral conceptions of atonement; and its commitment to make Christianity credible and socially relevant to modern people.

The appeal is primarily seen in imaginatively crafting a modern response to theology's changing face in order to keep the Christian theological message pertinent in society.

For Wilder, modernism and imagination were the newer angles through which Christian theology should be engaged.[8] He believed that this reformed approach would provide Christian theology with new energy and relevance.[9] But in responding from this space of unease, a particular theological voice was centered. The theological-liberalism crisis belonged to the most vocal bodies in the field: the White male ones. Wilder's message is partial at best; it only echoes the emerging liberalist theological concerns of his time.

Process theology scholars Roland Faber and Jeremy Fackenthal begin their edited anthology *Theopoetic Folds: Philosophizing Multifariousness* with the following offering: "Philosophic tradition has bestowed on us many beginnings in poetics and theopoetics."[10] Backing up this statement is their choice of source material: Greek literary tradition and philosophical tradition.

For Faber and Fackenthal, theopoetics dialogues with continental studies and the many, again often White and male, interlocutors found within this area of study. According to their framing, theopoetics has continental philosophical and process theological roots.[11] Their threefold definition of theopoetics echoes the principles set forth in Alfred Whitehead's notion of process theology. Since God is "poet," theopoetics is the "poetic of the poet"; it is the expression of life in process. Since God is not the only agent of the world's creative acts, theopoetics is the discourse that engages with this possibility. Finally, since God is spoken of as removed from the "plane of power," theopoetics is determined to avoid privileging power or forces like it.[12]

A familiar problem of access persists, however. The possibility for participation in such a conversation is unfortunately limited to process theology students and experts. Can theopoetics exist outside of these frames: exclusive academic locations, liberalist theological platforms, and philosophical silos? So far the conversation partners for "Traditional Theopoetics" have been White men. However, a feminist voice could potentially offer a different take.

Catherine Keller, a famed feminist process theologian and prevalent voice within theopoetic discourse, throws her theopoetic definition in the ring.

8. Wilder, "Theology and Theopoetic," 57. Wilder is careful to warn that imagination alone can become cultlike in itself. Imagination for imagination's sake "without roots, without tradition, without discipline."

9. Wilder, "Theology and Theopoetic," 7–8.

10. Roland Faber and Jeremy Fackenthal, eds., "Introduction: The Manifold of Theopoetics," in *Theopoetic Folds: Philosophizing Multifariousness* (New York: Fordham University Press, 2013), 1.

11. Faber and Fackenthal, "Introduction," 1–3.

12. Faber and Fackenthal, "Introduction," 4.

Speaking about progressive theopoetic beginnings near the end of her seminal work, *The Face of the Deep: A Theology of Becoming*, she states, "Talk about God: theology has been growing uncertain for centuries. Therein lies its great opportunity. It partakes little of the optimistic gleam of scientific progress, the insouciant originality of the arts. When for the sake of that sparkling novelty or that cultured public, religious thinkers dwell on the 'cutting edge,' they lose their traditional constituencies—and ipso facto, ironically, the activist potential that distinguishes progressive theology."[13]

According to Keller, theopoetics responds to the "uncertainty crisis" of Christian theology missing the opportunity to live into something different. Though aiming to explore how we think about God differently, Keller's work and approach feels very close to that used by Faber and Fackenthal. This is no coincidence. Keller considers herself part of the school of process theology, a branch of theological studies Dorrien argues to be "the leading, indeed 'the only vital school' of liberal progressive theology."[14] The liberalist concern feels tangible here. Keller's work seems to be in line with the concerns echoed in the works before hers—theology, traditionally understood, is losing its relevance. It needs to be saved. Theopoetics, then, seems to be the natural response for a world of thought feared to be dwindling toward insignificance.

PROBLEM AND POTENTIAL

What are you doing theopoetics for? *Who* are you doing theopoetics for?

While it is helpful to give an overview of how various White Western voices have considered theopoetics from their ontological context, questions of accessibility must be raised.

A liberalist approach to theopoetics works to prevent the decline of Christian theological relevance by employing imagination, and yet, another theopoetic angle has always coexisted from the space of imagination. But it has not been recognized until recently. Historically unable to access the spaces of Traditional Theopoetics, this powerful tool of the imagination has not been seen because it yields a different overarching message: liberation.

This other theopoetic angle is marginal but lives on. It is minoritized, but always creative—it has had to be in order for its peoples to survive. Like their

13. Catherine Keller, "Pneumatic Foam: Spirit Vibrating," in *The Face of the Deep: A Theology of Becoming* (New York: Routledge, 2003), 229.

14. Catherine Keller, "Theopoiesis and the Pluriverse: Notes on a Process," in Faber and Fackenthal, *Theopoetic Folds*, 180.

ecclesial parents, scholastic communities of color not privy to privileged theological circles create their own circles.

Less a scholastic category and more an embodied form of knowing, for marginalized communities, theopoetics is the space of how the self knows God. It is theologizing done amid the quest for spiritual and physical freedom. This is what I term "Theopoetics in Color."

Theopoetics in Color is tethered to a liberationist agenda, rather than a liberalist one. It emphasizes the wellness of a communal whole and braves creative approaches to God-talk and God-thought to do so. It is more accessible than a liberal-funded angle because it starts in and seeks the wellness of one's body, one's community, and one's people.

Theopoetics in Color is the freedom to do theological reflection from the space of one's body and all therein. Its conversation partners do not need theoretical or theological prowess or even a terminal degree to offer a rich contribution. Its language is simplistic and found in humble settings—in the quiet reflection of one's life experience, in exchanges at Bible studies, in chopping it up at kitchen tables, in parking lot conversations, on walks where wonder and curiosity collide, and in the shared stories nurtured in car rides. It is accessible because it is done everywhere. It is accessible because it is tangible to lives forgotten in the settings in which Traditional Theopoetics was and continues to be done. Theopoetics in Color is theopoetics that feels close—to one's body, to one's condition, to one's community. The theopoetic potential is both deeply rooted in bodies and communities and as expansive as the imaginations within those bodies and communities.

And yet, it has come to exist out of necessity. Because of its inability to bloom in traditional spaces—spaces that only take particular voices seriously within the theopoetics conversation—Theopoetics in Color has always already lived in communities cognizant of context.

Having a consciousness of who one is, and what this particularity means in the world of theopoetic inquiry, is critical. Keefe-Perry recalls the importance of acknowledging one's identity. He writes about how his colleague Patrick Reyes called him out on being unmindful of such details. Reyes signaled that in his book *Way to Water*, Keefe-Perry's approach to narrating theopoetic focal points and voices echoed a colonial framework, assuming a White and heteronormative male identity and perspective as the norm. It became clear that who Keefe-Perry *was* bled through in the structuring of what *he was calling and framing for others* as "theopoetics" and who *he* deemed worthy of doing theopoetics.[15]

---

15. L. Callid Keefe-Perry, "Alvesian Theopoetics, the Academy, and What May Come," *Literature and Theology* 33, no. 3 (September 2019): 321–35, esp. 324.

The whiteness and the maleness of his approach was not only personal, but also professional. Keefe-Perry admits that White male authors are always looked to for validation in many realms: an area of study, a theological opinion, a discourse, a person's credibility.[16]

Though he is a scholar fully cognizant of the colonial dangers of categories, Keefe-Perry's work limited the genesis narrative and ongoing existence of theopoetics in the world as primarily the thought exercise of White, male voices.

Amos Wilder, Roland Faber, Jeremy Fackenthal, Catherine Keller, and L. Callid Keefe-Perry can only speak from the space of who they are. This is not wrong; it is, however, limited.[17] In creating their work they lay the groundwork for what the theopoetics conversation sounds like and set the tone for who might be a part of the discourse in the future. And they do so with good intent—the impact, efficacy, and longevity of Christian theological discourse is at stake.

But the perspectival limits, problems with access, and intellectual practices of exclusivity of such thinkers do nothing to explore the range of theopoetic discourse.

You see the problem here. Liberal theological voices are not the same as liberationist ones. A liberal approach to theology is framed close to American identity—primarily male, primarily White. But everyone is not experiencing a crisis around preserving existing theological institutional relevance.

The urgency to revamp a theological approach speaks less to theology's presence in the world and more about its constituents. I initially called this mode of theopoetics WASP Theopoetics for a reason. A fight for theological relevance so rigorous that it demands different theological approaches reveals not only a particular worldview but a particular space taken up in that world. This is the problem.

Theopoetics, while historically treated as liberal theology's newest effort, is important because it is a diverse language of how one exists in the world—it is a way to speak one's being, one's life into existence in light of divine reflection. This is the potential.

---

16. L. Callid Keefe-Perry, "Alvesian Theopoetics," 321–35, esp. 324–25.

17. It is important to note that philosophical and theological areas such as process thought or phenomenology do have constituents and advocates of color. Voices like Monica Coleman utilize such approaches in their work. Such approaches can provide helpful frameworks toward liberationist agendas. What I am emphasizing is that these approaches should not constitute the sole or dominant face of what theopoetics is. The predominant and presupposed center within such discourses, White and male, is too often associated and thus called to name the form of theopoetics. This is, at best, an incomplete perspective.

The problem is limiting the space from which one does theopoetics to the small scope of anxious theological discourse. This aligns theopoetics with a mode of desperate intellectual survival. The potential is in seeing that theopoetics has existed in creative ways and as a creative force within the lives of those who understand survival in a different register.

Theopoetics solely constructed to breathe new life into stale discourse as an attempt at conjuring relevance is death-dealing; theopoetics uncovered from the folds of circumstances in which imagination and creativity are ancient sources of survival holds potential. It is a theological air that funds survival on a different front. This persistence, one concerned with joy and liberation and ultimately aimed at thriving, is life-giving.

Problem. Potential.

THEOPOETICS IN COLOR

Marginalized communities have a different relationship to theopoetics than what theological liberalism has put forth.

Theopoetics in minoritized communities is attached to a purpose: the freedom of its people. If disconnected from tangible action, theopoetics becomes lifeless thought exercise alone. Theopoetics that claims liberation and voice as survival, on the other hand, is weighty and substantive.

Again, we return to key questions for theopoetic discourse: *What* are you doing theopoetics for? *Who* are you doing theopoetics for?

Liberal theology fixated upon anxieties of relevance is inattentive to the liberative potential of theopoetics.

A liberationist bend to theopoetics seeks the material wellness of another, and the self. It is both imaginative and tangible. It is also global. It aspires to "construct a just and fraternal society, where persons can live with dignity and be the agents of their own destiny."[18]

Herein lies a point for consideration: Is theopoetics a liberal language of sorts? Though it attempts to be, I think not, for this argument rests upon Euro-Christian presuppositions[19] and, as we have seen with the ebb and flow of theopoetics' place in liberal circles, it loses its power, fast.

18. Gustavo Gutiérrez, "Introduction to the Original Edition," in *A Theology of Liberation: History, Politics, and Salvation* (Maryknoll, NY: Orbis Books: 1988), xiv.

19. Laurel Schneider, "The Gravity of Love: Theopoetics and Ontological Imagination," in Faber and Fackenthal, *Theopoetic Folds*, 113. Schneider makes the convincing case that "this assumption of an *originary pluralism* from which Christian theology properly begins, along with the mature awareness of the limitations of Euro-Christian modes of reasoning,

In contrast, Theopoetics in Color is more akin to a liberationist tongue. Its form and advocates are not Western and European in thought, voice, or experience. And further, a number of its constituents have known the essence of theopoetics prior to the language of process thought or philosophical theology. Many of its non-White, non-European devotees have known theopoetics in the communal practices of their families and communities, the language practices of their people, and the ideological creativity of their cultures. They do not *learn about* theopoetics but rather share with the world that which they already know that *finds voice in the category of theopoetics*. They speak of it from the work and wounds of their existence.

Though theopoetics signals a general idea of nonconformity, theological freedom for White scholars is not made of the same substance as it is for scholars from historically marginalized communities.

Theology itself, as a category, has been fraught for people of color.

For many of us minoritized scholars, the whiteness and maleness historically associated with theologizing has been the unfortunate foundation on which our understanding of our theological expertise has been built. We have had to unnecessarily perform the appropriate tricks of White Western canon memorization and expertise in order to even begin thinking and talking about the discourses that are close to our bodies and mean something to us.

Historically, we minoritized scholars have had to wait to address that which matters to and begins with us, that which has always been within us since the beginning. In theological study who we are has little to no space to come forth uninhibited, as our time and tongues are overcrowded with proving to various groups that we know the "forefathers" of our respective discourses of expertise.

But theopoetics done in color offers a liberating alternative. It opens the door for a new way of thinking. If we look at the timeline of theopoetics' emergence, one thing is clear: it has another beginning, a second genesis account. While it may look and be named differently, it has always been.

Stanley Hopper coined the term "theopoetics" in the same year Gustavo Gutiérrez coined the term "liberation theology."[20] Theopoetics as a term came to be known a year after James Cone's *Black Theology of Liberation* was released in 1970. In his 1968 dissertation, "Toward A Theology of Liberation," Rubem

---

form the primary set of presuppositions upon which a theopoetics of the manifold depends if it is actually to redress the deficits resident in dominant Christian theological reasoning today." She later argues that theopoetics not attentive to its plurality lacks humor and poetry and names numerous American indigenous voices critical to helping her understand the form of theopoetic multiplicity.

20. See Gustavo Gutiérrez, *A Theology of Liberation: History, Politics, and Salvation* (Maryknoll, NY: Orbis Books: 1988).

Alves first spoke of a theology of liberation (three years before Gutiérrez made mention of it).[21]

To be clear, I am not calling these discourses categorically theopoetic, but what I am saying is that these angles of theology are theopoetic. They do creative God-reflection from the space of the body and toward the totality of liberation. Theopoetics is the *nature* of a theological sound, the aspirational means by which one can do one's theologically reflective work.

For minoritized communities, theopoetics is theological inquiry by a different name.

Once its focus is turned away from anxious preservation toward liberation, theopoetics can be recognized as already having a lifespan within the theological expression of the marginalized.

Liberation theologies—its Latinx, Latina feminist, *mujerista*, Black, Black feminist, womanist, African, African feminist, Asian, Asian-American, Asian feminist, American indigenous, and queer and quare spokes—and other liberative theological forms, such as postcolonial and decolonial theologies, persist in the theopoetic charge. They have *always* persisted in the theopoetic charge!

Those who lack the cognizance to see the wrinkles of theopoetics in the faces of liberationist and minority-centered modes of scholarship must look again. Those unaware of how long theopoetics has been in the bones of minoritized theologies and communal practices are tasked to recognize its antiquity. It might merely be another name for that which marginalized voices have been saying and doing theology for decades—centuries, even.

Though White Anglo-Saxon Protestant thinkers may have been some of the first voices to *publish* thoughts on theopoetics, *doing* Theopoetics in Color has been a historical practice of liberation by many.

Theopoetics in Color has many features and is many things: liberationist, decolonial, open to pluralistic conversation, free-formed or connected to ecclesial contexts, and intersectional. It invokes literature, cultural studies, postcolonial and decolonial studies, politics, linguistics, theology, and all modes of art—from playwriting, visual art, and film to photography, poetry, and more.

To choose to ignore this other genesis, and its multivalent theological reach, is practicing obliviousness at best, and ethnocentrism at worst.

To prevent theopoetics from becoming the newest instantiation of a colonial-based theological and philosophical project, we pay attention to and honor these multiple forms of theopoetic beginnings.

---

21. L. Callid Keefe-Perry, "Renewal and Nets," in *Way to Water*, 42–43, esp. n38. Keefe-Perry makes this keen observation about the date of Alves's work.

This project is a beginning of sorts. It features minoritized voices asking: Who gets to tell us about the veracity of our God-framing? And it answers: we do, however we need to.

This work, *Theopoetics in Color*, does not ask for permission or affirmation that we are doing theopoetics correctly. Instead, our posture in this work is one of collectively showing you, telling you, reminding you that it is so.

Chapter Overviews

Theopoetics in Color is a project committed to honoring and hearing from marginalized sources, voices, and places. The aim is to expand the concept of "source." The hope is to let theopoetics be as expansive as it actually is. The goal is for theopoetics to be accessible and recognizable.

Theopoetics in Color is the first text of its kind to illuminate diverse voices within and approaches to theopoetics, redirecting the discourse toward the form that feels truest to us: imaginative theological reflection toward liberation.[22] This work demonstrates that theopoetics is, in fact, a colorful exercise.[23]

In this text, thirteen distinct and prominent voices offer modern approaches to doing theopoetics in four sections:[24] "Performance and Voice," illuminating the aesthetic and creative reach of theopoetics; "Methods and Inquiries," granting minoritized voices space to show their read of theopoetic

---

22. A point worth mentioning: the majority of the voices found within this anthology will be speaking from a Christian theological or Christian theologizing perspective. This is a shortcoming of this project. Should this project or another like it in content or spirit emerge, the hope is to honor the pluralistic approach we know that theopoetics can and does take.

23. I have intentionally not provided a referential definition of "theopoetics" with which the authors of this project will be working. It is not mine to monolithically define and thus hold some sort of false claim over. It is all of ours to unveil how we see fit and how we have known it through our lives, in our imaginations, and through our being in the world, thus our respective definitions of "theopoetics" will unfold either directly or indirectly in our respective chapters.

24. The creation of this project is organic and is not aiming to meet any type of diversity criteria. In assembling this project, I have not pursued some type of representational checklist concerning demographics around race and ethnicity (except that authors must be from a minoritized ethnic group), gender, class, age, sexual orientation, occupation, denominational foundation, political view, etc. that the authors must meet for *Theopoetics in Color*. The spirit of this work is to grant each author space to constructively do their own work, naming and showing what theopoetics looks like and means *for them*, without being tokenized or marked for diversity purposes. This open "method" embodies a liberative approach to content building that we hope this work itself will do, in turn.

methodological approach; "Interlocutors," detailing conversation partners of and subsequent conversations in theopoetics; and, finally, "Hermeneutics, Proclamation, and Claim," examining the place and practice of theopoetic imagination in everyday circumstances.

Part 1, "Performance and Voice," opens up with questions about the placement and movement of minoritized bodies and how they might grant theopoetic access. In chapter 1, Patrick B. Reyes offers a Chicano futurist exploration of theological voice and imagination. He resists colonial performance of subjectivity and consecrates plane travel; he invites the reader to imagine with him how subversive space can be sacralized and new worlds can be envisioned. In chapter 2, Lis Valle-Ruiz explores playwriting as an embodied source for doing theopoetics in her self-written play, *Words and Flesh, Entangled.* She argues that movement and interaction are often-overlooked locations of theopoetic formation. In chapter 3, Lakisha R. Lockhart-Rusch resists the charge to "sound White" in order for her voice to be validated in the academy. Instead, Lockhart-Rusch interrogates how and why the academy is a space lacking a sense of wholeness; she charges its members to undo colonial binds and help cocreate a space affirming human wellness.

Part 2, "Methods and Inquiries," tackles head-on the question of how one might characterize the methodology of theopoetics based on one's social location and critical aims. In chapter 4, Tiffany U. Trent argues against disembodied research when employing a theopoetic lens. This nuanced angle impacts not only the collection of data but also data's content. In chapter 5, Tamisha A. Tyler outlines what a four-part inclusive theopoetic framework looks like for her through conversation with themes in the work of Octavia Butler. In chapter 6, Carolina Hinojosa-Cisneros interrogates collective imagination within the Latinx community through the theopoetic epistemology of Gloria Anzaldúa. She outlines theopoetic "knowing" as impacting one's learning and inclination to act justly.

Part 3, "Interlocutors," gives a snapshot of theopoetic conversation through interlocutors outside the field of religious studies. In chapter 7, Yohana Agra Junker engages Latin American visual artist Doris Salcedo, whose narrative work parallels the theopoetic striving toward voice and liberation. In chapter 8, James Howard Hill Jr. explores the complicated and interpersonal entanglement of divinized figureheads as he converses with prior iterations of his own father-son relationship. In chapter 9, Peace Pyunghwa Lee explores how Black queer photographer Alvin Baltrop demonstrates theopoetic attention to the sacredness of marginalized bodies through his artistic practices of recognition. In chapter 10, in conversation with the critical essayist and poet Audre Lorde,

Oluwatomisin Olayinka Oredein

Oluwatomisin Olayinka Oredein queries the process of selecting theopoetic interlocutors and how to best honor the insights their work offers.

Part 4, "Hermeneutics, Proclamation, and Claim," puts theopoetic interpretation into practice through cultural hermeneutics. Here, these voices proclaim and claim theopoetic interpretive practice as their own and as belonging to their communities. In chapter 11, Joyce del Rosario argues the communal space and practices of Filipino potlucks are theological repositories. In chapter 12, Yara González-Justiniano explores how linguistic sayings within the Latinx community, when interpreted through a theopoetic lens, are sites of theological wisdom and insight. In chapter 13, Brian Bantum puts flesh to theopoetic Christian systematic theology by proposing an asystematic lens and approach.

Theopoetics in Color treats the self as a contextual source of divine reflection and insight. Its authors take up the challenge of the question: How does one *do* theopoetics? We speak of God from the space of our specific embodiment and experiences. Our experience of God is theological source; we learn and understand God through our bodies.

So, why theopoetics? Why *Theopoetics in Color*? Because we trust ourselves, but more so, we trust that divine revelation is not thought exercise alone but is found in paying attention to the wonder of how we materially and actually lead a life in this world.

WHAT YOU WILL GET IN THIS BOOK

Through this collection of essays and voices, my colleagues and I are trying to do theopoetics without pretense and undue pressure, without unnecessary categorical rigidity. We *have* put a name to the religious reflection and theologizing we are doing; we unashamedly name it theopoetics. But we see theopoetics as a part of our language, not our entire vocabulary—for we know that voice is more complicated than that!

We are theopoets because our voices and insights bend toward liberation. The traces of what our races and ethnicities have meant in this world have made their way into our words, thought processes, and respective imaginations. Our God-talk spans and outlasts waves of religious reflection and God-talk that have tried to construct gates around the "best" and proper expressions of itself. We do not do gates. We do passageways, and avenues, and different ways of free movement. Our words are moving; our ideas are always in motion. We are actively holding the ideas in the past in tension with the realities we are seeing today and putting word, verse, visual, audio, and affect to them. We are writing our freedom, theologizing what an unmarked, boundless heart can be. We do not have the capacity to *not* speak from a space of liberative truth. Truth is our language; and we hope that in our telling the truth and sharing what we know, have seen, and are seeing now that we provide a roadmap to free expression; for free expression is one means of living as a liberated soul. Theopoetics in color invites the complicated truth into our respective homes and asks her to stay a while, for we intend to live with her for quite a while.

We intend to live.

Works Cited

Dorrien, Gary. "Modernisms in Theology: Interpreting American Liberal Theology, 1805–1950." *American Journal of Theology & Philosophy* 23, no. 3 (September 2002): 200–220.

Faber, Roland, and Jeremy Fackenthal, eds. *Theopoetic Folds: Philosophizing Multifariousness*. New York: Fordham University Press, 2013.

Gutiérrez, Gustavo. *A Theology of Liberation: History, Politics, and Salvation*. Maryknoll, NY: Orbis Books: 1988.

Keefe-Perry, L. Callid. "Alvesian Theopoetics, the Academy, and What May Come." *Literature and Theology* 33, no. 3 (September 2019): 321–35.

———. "Renewal and Nets." In Keefe-Perry, *Way to Water*, 32–50.

———. *Way to Water: A Theopoetics Primer*. Eugene, OR: Cascade, 2014.

Keller, Catherine. *The Face of the Deep: A Theology of Becoming*. New York: Routledge, 2003.

———. "Pneumatic Foam: Spirit Vibrating." In *The Face of the Deep*, chapter 14.

———. "Theopoiesis and the Pluriverse: Notes on a Process." In Faber and Fackenthal, *Theopoetic Folds*, 179–94.

Placher, William C., ed. *Essentials of Christian Theology*. Louisville: Westminster John Knox, 2003.

Schneider, Laurel. "The Gravity of Love: Theopoetics and Ontological Imagination." In Faber and Fackenthal, *Theopoetic Folds*, 109–123.

Valentine, Benjamin. *In Our Own Voices: Latino/a Renditions of Theology*. Maryknoll, NY: Orbis Books, 2010.

Wilder, Amos. *Theopoetic: Theology and the Religious Imagination*. Lima, OH: Academic Renewal Press, 2001.

Part 1

PERFORMANCE AND VOICE

1

Cyborgs and Future Wars

A Revolutionary's Guide to Living in Liberation

PATRICK B. REYES

They tried to take our gods, then they remade them in their own image.
 They erased our memories, replacing them with their own.
 They tore down our buildings and built monuments to their empire on top.

Cyborgs

They stole our tongues, inserting their language in our heads.
 They severed our connection to the land, displacing and disrupting our practices of following the hummingbirds and butterflies, the rivers, and the mountains.
 They put us to work, to maintain their destruction of our people, our place, our purpose.
 We became cyborgs, traveling on artificial roads, speaking, reading, writing in unfamiliar tones and sounds. We could still feel the remnants of a land not quite lost below our feet, guided by the gods of old.
 For every generation the challenge has been to survive. Replacing parts of their bodies, as all cyborgs can purchase new parts on the colonial market-place, some believe they can gain access to empire's version of humanity. There are others who have learned to be of value in this destruction, displacement,

and denial. They serve only to remove any remnants of our world. There are those cyborgs among us who sit in the libraries, archives, and universities erasing memories on behalf of them: mimicking their stories, correcting records that managed to survive the fires. There will always be cyborgs, ready to play chaplain to the destroyer and condemn the resistance, serving gods they can neither hear, see, nor touch.

Among the cyborgs though, there are a few who dream of new worlds. A few freedom fighters actively resist, who instead of replacing their parts, are removing them, leaving open scars and seeking out medicine to heal. There are cyborgs among us who have returned to the land to explore harmony and balance. Here they know that the underground rivers will never run dry, and they lead to those places of life, the subterranean villages where our ancestors dance and play. There are those among us who are writing in secret, sometimes in those very places where the records are being destroyed, preserving and resurrecting our histories, traditions, and people. They manage to see their parts as augmentations necessary to their survival—the survival of their body and the bodies that came before. An even smaller group among us can leave these mutilated bodies all together, to go to the plane of the gods, to take rest, to seek guidance, and to learn the spiritual teachings from the first beings. This group is neither ordained nor certified in this world.

When we came to understand that we were a network of freedom fighters, resisting the mutilation to our bodies, lands, and histories, we began to forge new relations, new ways of being together. There were many terms that could have captured it, and let us be clear, theopoetics fails miserably at capturing the spirit and soul of the people who work within its limitations. But it gave a place, familiar and unthreatening to those who sought to destroy us and undefined enough to allow us to imagine new. Or, is it old? Or, is it something unstuck in time?

We must be vigilant. Agents of destruction are everywhere. Even in this new space, we would find those who want to control, define, or as the agents of empire might say: "We are here to learn." It is all the same to us because their ends were always our ends. The means, as they said, were to end us. They take those parts of us they desire, those parts that they fetishize, and they graft it onto their own bodies, adorning themselves with the pieces we will never recover. It is their way of "celebrating" or "supporting" us. Pillage and plunder can look like the power of proximity.

Our status never changes from high alert. As Baldwin said: "In a society that is entirely hostile, and, by its nature, seems determined to cut you down— that has cut down so many in the past and cuts down so many every day—it begins to be almost impossible to distinguish a real from a fancied injury. One can very quickly cease to attempt this distinction, and what is worse, one usually ceases to attempt it without realizing that one has done so."[1] It is not paranoia, if post traumatic slave condition(s), terror management theory, and evidence of coloniality are to be believed—and I do believe them. Cyborgs pass memory and terror from one generation to the next, through parts that we neither desire nor wanted and, at times, we cannot control. Those parts foreign to us can take over and flood the system with the screams of our ancestors and the cries of our descendants.

Meanwhile, they sit in their towers of knowledge, justifying their violence, saying they need to preserve their history and knowledge. They use words like "imagining anew" or "reform." In large libraries and institutions, they say their cultures are under attack. Their fiction always includes tomes about how the end times will include the burning of their books, their places of education, worship, and culture. This imagination comes not from an unrealized future, but from their realized past. They burned our books. They destroyed our places of education, worship, and culture. What they fear most is that we will treat them the way they treated us.

What are we to do then, we cyborgs committed to freedom? There is no returning this body to its pure state. There is no future where extraction and expulsion are determined by them.

Is there?

Can we dream of a world where the beauty of healing outweighs the pain of removing these parts that rot our flesh? There is no doubt this will require healing. Theopoetics, though limited and bound by even those theorists who seek to erase us, provides a small outpost in intellectual empire. A small place where cyborgs can come to play, imagine, create, define, resist, and rest with limited exposure to the violence of empire.

In its best form, we can reimagine and reclaim our gods.

We can recover memory. Where the Sankofa bird meets Huitzilopochtli.

We can go to those spaces beyond man-built structures and rejoice in the temples of the gods.

We can reclaim our many tongues, writing as the poets, priests, and prophets once did.

We can work for our people and our way of being.

---

1. James Baldwin, "Letter from a Region in My Mind," *New Yorker*, November 9, 1962, https://www.newyorker.com/magazine/1962/11/17/letter-from-a-region-in-my-mind.

Patrick B. Reyes

Planes

There are several ways to get to the next plane. For the cyborgs among us, the spiritualists, those connected to the ancestors, one way is to recover that which has been extracted. There is a strand of writing where practice drives: making art, research, and exploration of the imagination as those who walked this planet before this time. They find beauty in the magical and mundane alike. The spiritual plane is not separate from the material world; rather, there is a mesh that has been placed on this world by those who sought to colonize it. Their violence shrouded, even from them, the sights, the smells, the sounds, the tastes, the feeling of the spiritual and ancestral planes. The cyborgs who seek to create this connection imagine worlds in this world. Talking trees, be-friending animal life, listening streams and oceans, this plane is for those who can pay deep attention to the ways the fairies, the great forest spirit Shishigami (シシガミ), the Ents,[2] the great whales who live alongside the mycelium tracking the history of this planet, recording their wisdom in the archives of their ever-expanding network.

Some of us dream of worlds beyond worlds. We find more in the imagination off this planet than here. Here the world of science is less fiction and more exploration. Here the future of the world is not disconnected from the spiritual plane; it is rather where they connect. They are the worlds imagined by Octavia Butler or Grace Dillon in *Walking the Clouds*.[3] Speculative imagination allows worlds where our connection to spirit and technology is one of relationship not unlike Gundam.[4] Sometimes it will be a connection with others and relationship across races, only amplified by the way that we connect to form Voltron. Even Battlestar Galactica had their spiritual traditions. This off-planet imagination is an exploration to transcend the violent world we, cyborgs, have survived.

The spiritual plane is for the speculative. It is for those like Octavia Butler, Kim Stanley Robinson, Donna Barba Higuera, N. K. Jemisin, and Cixin Liu.[5]

2. J. R. R. Tolkien, *The Two Towers* (London: Grafton, 1991).

3. Grace L. Dillon, "Imagining Indigenous Futurisms," in *Walking the Clouds: An Anthology of Indigenous Science Fiction*, ed. Grace L. Dillon (Tucson: University of Arizona Press, 2012), 1–12.

4. Yoshikazu Yasuhiko, *Mobile Suit Gundam: The Origin* (New York: Vertical Comics, 2013).

5. Octavia E. Butler, *Parable of the Sower* (New York: Grand Central, 2000); Butler, *Parable of the Talents* (New York: Grand Central, 2019); Kim Stanley Robinson, *The Ministry for the Future: A Novel* (London: Orbit, 2020); Donna Barba Higuera, *The Last Cuentista*

World-building requires an acute sense of what is and what will be. Speculative writers, though, provide a view into the interior life as well as the world. Cyborgs, future dwellers, or those who cross time have deep interior lives. They prompt us to imagine, What if? The turn to dwell in a world we built is to build an interior life that explores the depths of our souls. Love, connection, belonging—these are all central to world-building. Just as those great writers built worlds beyond worlds, we build interior worlds.

The building of interior worlds is no easier than building them in the material world. The violence done to the body can seep like poison into the mind. One's medicine bag is not just for the material plane. We must take our tokens, medicines, and prayers with us to the spiritual plane. We must practice as the ancestors have taught us.

Howard Thurman, Alice Walker, Rubem Alves,[6] and contemporary mystics remind us to return to the interior life. Below the wiring, there is still a full human connected to the divine. This exploration of the interior life is one that rarely has the language of intellectual empire. It provides access to everyone, because while it might start with the spiritual, it always ends with the individual. That is, if you read it incorrectly.

The challenge for us who seek freedom in the interior life: those great teachers who came before us left secret codes in their writings and teachings, calling out the injustice. A spiritual fast is not a rejection of the living body. On the outside it looks like a spiritual discipline only. A commitment to a stoic mind over body. But a fast, in its best expression, is deeply connected with the body. It is a cleansing of the body.

A fast is a refusal to feed the parts placed on us by empire.

In the body, a spiritual fast is a revolution against the religion of empire.

It is as much a spiritual practice as it is the refusal to give energy to the demands against us. Cultivating the inner life is about finding the space where we can dream of worlds not inhabited by colonization. It is in the connection to the inner divine, a space that empire and agents of empire do not have ac-

(Montclair: Levine Querido, 2021); N. K. Jemisin, *The Fifth Season* (New York: Orbit, 2015); Cixin Liu, *The Three-Body Problem* (New York: Tom Doherty, 2016).

6. Howard Thurman, *Jesus and the Disinherited* (Boston: Beacon, 1996); Thurman, *For the Inward Journey: The Writings of Howard Thurman* (New York: Harcourt Brace Jovanovich, 1984); Thurman, *Deep Is the Hunger* (Richmond, IN: Friends United, 1978); Alice Walker, *In Search of Our Mothers' Gardens: Womanist Prose* (Orlando: Mariner Books, 2003); Rubem Alves, *Tomorrow's Child: Imagination, Creativity, and the Rebirth of Culture* (Eugene, OR: Wipf & Stock, 2011); Alves, *Poet, the Warrior, the Prophet* (London: Hymns Ancient & Modern, 2002).

cess to, that we can find freedom. Fasting refuses the energy demands of our colonial parts. It is world-building and dreaming. It is a way of cultivating the space where we can hear the ancestors guiding our hands and feet as we construct the cultural and spiritual resilience to survive. My inner sanctuary cannot be colonized. In the Holy of Holies, there we will meet the divine.

Awake

When we woke up, we knew there had to be another way. We all saw each other. We could hear our ancestors singing. We could see the ship to take us off-world. We were connecting soul to soul. No words were spoken. Our inner and outer worlds were connected by the *god of change*. From Aztlán to Acorn, with guides like Rudolfo Anaya,[7] and Yoshikazu Yasuhiko and Yoshiyuki Tomino (the creators of Gundam), we will write with Slave in Utero, climbing the *Tower of God* that does not serve us and refusing to take each of their tests, restoring relationship between the human and nonhuman.[8]

There is a war for life. A war for belonging, between those who want to save life and those who want to take it. It is not enough to be included in their worlds as cyborgs, the mechanization of empire. It is a war of imagination. The struggle to orient the spiritual back to the natural. Among us freedom fighters, some will resist by removing all those parts, seeking healing, and helping others find awakening. Here the awakening, the healing, the training, is learning to be frontline scouts, medics, healers, and teachers. They will master all four elements and go between planes, meeting with spirits, and are themselves multispirit beings. They find ways to love deeply, to explore bodies with right relation and respect. Some of us will develop a new way forward, connecting with technologies only imagined by empire. Technologies developed by our ancestors. Calendars that signal our time to rise and mathematics that lead to the calculations that drive our mechs, our tools of resistance.

Prophetesses and warriors will continue to unlock new tools and practices to directly confront empire and redefine our relationship to its citizens. And finally, there will be those among us who will simply survive on empire's edge. They will preserve and transmit our knowledges, because they know wars are

7. Rudolfo A. Anaya, *The Essays* (Norman: University of Oklahoma Press, 2009); Anaya, *Bless Me, Ultima* (Rockland, MA: Wheeler, 2008).
8. Slave in Utero, "[Season 1] Ep. 0 | Tower of God," Webtoon, June 30, 2014, https://www.webtoons.com/en/fantasy/tower-of-god/season-1-ep-0/viewer?title_no=95&episode_no=1.

not fought and won on this timeline but are those who see time bending back on itself. The mystics find ways to see the longer arc when the conflict for life will see enemies as allies, where the lines between the good and the bad are already blurred because they do not see pure histories or futures. Theopoetics might be a place where our strategies are created. For this shaman of words, it provides a place to offer clues and pathways to freedom. It will not be where the world is created new, but where curanderos might place symbols, like those often found above doors: EXIT. It may be where we commit to the following cyborg spiritual disciplines.

CYBORG SPIRITUAL DISCIPLINES

1. **Resistance**. The sake of the planet, your cousins, and future generations depend on us finding pathways to freedom. The school of the cyborgs and mystics still needs to be built. You are who we have been waiting for—the school, the generation, who can resist empire. The ancestors survived so you may resist.

2. **Revolution**. Commit to spiritual revolution that resists purity narratives. World-building demands that we find ways to commit to bringing about the revolution that frees us from the parts placed on us by empire. Revolution of the heart and soul is necessary. The religious pacemaker forces an irregular heartbeat. Revolution requires that we unplug and return to the rhythm of the waters and winds, the breaths of the world around us.

3. **Rest**. Rest is resistance. Rest is revolution. Spiritual rest is necessary to shed the pieces placed on our bodies by empire. The only way to free us from cages and limitations placed on the imagination is to rest. Empire desires your labor. They augment your body for labor. To rest is not to prepare for further exploitation but to center the need to recover from generations of spiritual exhaustion and colonial violence.

4. **Reap**. Reap not everything, but what nourishes the community. Choose to leave what is not necessary. Cultivate the generational wisdom that will give our descendants the nourishment and seeds they need to plant the communities of resistance, revolution, and rest we need.

5. **Remember**. Re-member, re-place, reimagine yourself connected to a line of spiritual warriors, prophets, mystics, priests, lovers, and survivors. Tell the story again and again. The dramas and comedies, tales and legends, myths and narratives are all necessary for future generations to imagine their worlds. The gift of stories of resistance, revolution, rest, and reaping

traditions from within our communities will build a future world that will not rely on empire.

Resistance. Revolution. Rest. Reap. Remember. I commit my life to the five cyborg spiritual disciplines.

> To make a world, we must unmake the world.
> God of change, protect us as we commit to finding freedom.
> Deliver us,
> From this world to the next.

Will we realize these new worlds? In the end, the gods will have to decide. The decisions are not between the old gods and new. Instead, the gods will choose their beloved as they always have. We can imagine we are in the number and that our many mothers will choose to love us. For this cyborg, keeper of the waters and wind, it is not just the gods' decision. Their fate, their existence, also rests in our hands. For without us, what are they?

Works Cited

Alves, Rubem. *Poet, the Warrior, the Prophet*. London: Hymns Ancient & Modern, 2002.

———. *Tomorrow's Child: Imagination, Creativity, and the Rebirth of Culture*. Eugene, OR: Wipf & Stock, 2011.

Anaya, Rudolfo. *Bless Me, Ultima*. Rockland, MA: Wheeler, 2008.

———. *The Essays*. Norman: University of Oklahoma Press, 2009.

Baldwin, James. "Letter from a Region in My Mind." *New Yorker*, November 9, 1962. https://www.newyorker.com/magazine/1962/11/17/letter-from-a-region-in-my-mind.

Butler, Octavia E. *Parable of the Sower*. New York: Grand Central, 2000.

———. *Parable of the Talents*. New York: Grand Central, 2019.

Dillon, Grace L. "Imagining Indigenous Futurisms." In *Walking the Clouds: An Anthology of Indigenous Science Fiction*, edited by Grace L. Dillon, 1–12. Tucson: University of Arizona Press, 2012.

Higuera, Donna Barba. *The Last Cuentista*. Montclair: Levine Querido, 2021.

Jemisin, N. K. *The Fifth Season*. New York: Orbit, 2015.

Liu, Cixin. *The Three-Body Problem*. New York: Tom Doherty, 2016.

Robinson, Kim Stanley. *The Ministry for the Future: A Novel*. London: Orbit, 2020.

Slave in Utero. "[Season 1] Ep. 0 | Tower of God." Webtoon. June 30, 2014. https://www.webtoons.com/en/fantasy/tower-of-god/season-1-ep-0/viewer?title_no=95&episode_no=1.

Thurman, Howard. *Deep Is the Hunger*. Richmond, IN: Friends United, 1978.

———. *For the Inward Journey: The Writings of Howard Thurman*. New York: Harcourt Brace Jovanovich, 1984.

———. *Jesus and the Disinherited*. Boston: Beacon, 1996.

Tolkien, J. R. R. *The Two Towers*. London: Grafton, 1991.

Walker, Alice. *In Search of Our Mothers' Gardens: Womanist Prose*. Orlando: Mariner Books, 2003.

Yasuhiko, Yoshikazu. *Mobile Suit Gundam: The Origin*. New York: Vertical Comics, 2013.

2

Fleshly Theopoetics

Performance as Resistance in the Theological Academy

LIS VALLE-RUIZ

My body has a voice. My body communicates. It is true that I can use my body to express claims that I have thoughtfully crafted. It is also true that I can thoughtfully listen to the claims of my body. In my body and in other people's bodies I find ancient wisdom received subconsciously through performance. Performance transfers embodied knowledge from generation to generation.[1] Bodies transfer genetic knowledge and cultural and generational memory.[2]

When I seek my body's wisdom, I do my best to stop thinking. My goal is to bracket cognition and set aside reason. Rather, I let my body move. I open myself to a different epistemology, to embodied knowledge. I do my best to stop thinking intellectually and instead think bodily (with my body instead

1. On the transference of knowledge through performance, see the work of the American performance theorist and professor at New York University, who grew up in Mexico, Diana Taylor, *The Archive and the Repertoire: Performing Cultural Memory in the Americas* (Durham, NC: Duke University Press, 2003).

2. There is a growing body of research on how stressful and traumatic experiences alter how DNA is transferred to offspring, a phenomenon that psychology understands as generational transference of traumatic memory. See research on epigenetic memory. For example, Agustina D'Urso and Jason H. Brickner, "Mechanisms of Epigenetic Memory," *Trends in Genetics* 30, no. 6 (June 2014): 230–36. See also Tim Stephens, "Study Shows How Epigenetic Memory Is Passed across Generations," *UC Santa Cruz News*, September 18, 2014, https://news.ucsc.edu/2014/09/epigenetics.html.

of my mind). I pay attention to the "voice" of my body. I do not tell my body what to communicate. When I write from bodily wisdom, I do not reflect a posteriori on a prior embodied experience. Rather, I let my body (or other people's bodies) tell me what I (or we) need to communicate.[3] Our bodies generate fleshly theopoetics. That is how my play *Words & Flesh Entangled* came to be.

This essay came to be in a different way. Using newly acquired academic language, I share a story of how a minoritized student, filled with both intelligence and creativity, communicates through theopoetics, while the academy knows only the language of grandiose and often inaccessible words. Compelled by felt necessity in this approach, these pages emerge from a posteriori reflection on a prior embodied experience. This essay tells the story of a student in a PhD program in homiletics and liturgics who communicated her dissertation thesis bodily. I share this story to illustrate the conflict that arises from the cultural clash between student and institution, colonized and colonizing logics, theopoetics and phallogocentrism (the primacy of both the masculine and of language in the construction of meaning). The point of sharing this is to show that the only language that the academy speaks and writes, hears and reads, is words. Here, "the academy" is both the specific place where this story takes place, that is, the Graduate Department of Religion of Vanderbilt University in Nashville, Tennessee, and the schools of higher theological education in general. Later reflection on the experience of using an embodied approach to do theology in color as a doctoral student in the academy provided wisdom to develop this proposal for fleshly theopoetics.

The Play *Words & Flesh Entangled*

Words & Flesh Entangled is a play that I devised (facilitated by a collaborative process of creation), directed, and presented on May 4, 2018, at All Faith Chapel, Vanderbilt University, Nashville, Tennessee.[4] The play integrates what I learned during my doctoral program and the research conducted for my doctoral dissertation. The play expresses my thesis through physical and ex-

---

3. I learned this creative process during my undergraduate studies in the course *Brincos y Saltos*. See Rosa Luisa Márquez, *Brincos y saltos: El juego como disciplina teatral; Ensayos y manual de teatreros ambulantes* (Cayey, PR: Ediciones Cuicaloca con el Co-auspicio del Colegio Universitario de Cayey, 1992).

4. "Devising" is a collaborative process for generating a work of theater. See for example, Joan Schirle, "Potholes in the Road to Devising," *Theatre Topics* 15, no. 1 (March 2005): 91–102.

perimental theater rather than realism.[5] It is structured in two acts, the first consists of five scenes and the second of three scenes. The script is conceived for one actress/actor (hereinafter, referred to as "actor" or "actress") and volunteers from the audience. The actress represents two aspects of the same being: WORDS and FLESH. The actor switches from one aspect to the other by turning around a liturgical stole, beige on one side to represent FLESH, and aqua on the other side to represent WORDS.

The play develops in Aristotelian fashion, with introduction, development, climax, and resolution. The play presents a preacher whose WORDS fight his FLESH until WORDS kicks out FLESH from the pulpit and chancel. FLESH comes back with a bunch of prophets protesting. FLESH and WORDS fight again until they split open the preacher's liturgical stole. From within the stole, various liturgical stoles come out in different colors. Each prophet takes one. All the characters sit down for a eucharistic picnic while the preacher processes the situation. Each prophet brings a different item for the picnic and the play ends with all the characters seated in a semicircle showing through the stoles the colors of the rainbow and enjoying a sacramental meal with the audience who has been seated in a semicircle all along. Actors and spect-actors form a full circle.[6]

The reader of this essay may want to know what the play means. However, this essay is not about the play's content. Withholding the meaning of the play

---

5. Physical theater and experimental theater are part of the avant-garde. Physical theater uses the body and movement to tell a story. It encourages improvisation, is interdisciplinary, uses little to no dialogue, and likes breaking the fourth wall to incorporate active participation from the audience. See, for example, Diep Tran, "What Is Physical Theater?," *Backstage Magazine*, last updated April 18, 2022, https://www.backstage.com/magazine/article/physical-theater-guide-74965/. Experimental theater challenges how to write, produce, rehearse, and present bourgeois theater. It got rid of the proscenium arch, explored different relationships between actors and audience, challenged the hierarchical way of writing and directing plays, and sought to change or create new culture and intervene politically. See, for example, Christopher Innes, *Avant Garde Theatre: 1892–1992* (London: Routledge, 1993). Realism is theater that reflects daily living as it is; it mirrors society. The sets and costumes are no longer stylized but rather quotidian places and clothes of normal people, the themes are those affecting the lives of common citizens. The language is not poetry or rhyming verses like in past theater styles or genres but colloquial. See, for example, Carmina Aredez, "El teatro realista y sus características más destacadas," Espectáculos BCN, September 21, 2020, https://www.espectaculosbcn.com/teatro-realista-caracteristicas/.

6. "Spect-actors" is a term developed by Brazilian theater practitioner and theorist Augusto Boal. It refers to the spectators becoming active participants in a theater forum as they create dramatic action. See Augusto Boal, *Theatre of the Oppressed*, trans. Charles A. and Maria-Odilia Leal McBride (New York: Theatre Communications, 1985).

for those who did not understand it will keep our attention on what matters here, that the academy is monolingual and its only language is words. Such an ethos reveals that the academy is phallogocentric. Phallogocentrism is not the only way. Another world is possible, and fleshly theopoetics can perform the picture for us.

PHALLOGOCENTRISM IN THE ACADEMY

The academy is steeped in Western culture and its phallogocentric systems of thought. "Phallogocentric" is a term that combines two concepts, phallocentric and logocentric. Phallocentric refers to any system that gives primacy to the penis or is centered around the phallus.[7] Logocentric refers to the Western philosophical stance of privileging speech over writing and prioritizing rational thought (245). Algerian-French philosopher Jacques Derrida developed the concept, as professor of English (presumably American from the United States)[8] Mary Klages (217) explains, "The idea that words—'in the beginning was the word'—are a primary creative force is what Derrida calls logocentrism; logos meaning 'word' or sometimes logic, and centrism meaning 'at the center.'" Derrida critiqued French psychoanalyst and psychiatrist Jacques Lacan, calling him phallogocentric because Lacan named the phallus as the center of the symbolic order and the source and origin of language (257). French philosopher Hélène Cixous and poststructuralist feminists also critique phallogocentric Western philosophy for shaping a culture structured by binary oppositions subordinating the feminine to the masculine (67, 257). In this essay, then, I understand phallogocentrism as the centering of male ways of thinking and being and positioning words (as they know it) as the supreme expression of rational logic.

The academy lives into phallogocentric systems of thought. It has been privileging rational thought, words, and rational logic, as well as male ways of thinking and being ever since Plato founded his school of philosophy in the fourth century BCE. His students were men, Athenian, property owners, Greek-speaking, and idle (as opposed to engaged in work, like enslaved peo-

---

7. Mary Klages, *Literary Theory: The Complete Guide* (London: Bloomsbury Academic, 2017), 257, Kindle. Hereafter, references to this source will appear in the text.

8. I add "from the United States" to remind ourselves that "America" has many countries other than the United States. Subsequent occurrences describing an individual from the United States will appear as "US American."

ple). Their social location allowed them to be academics: "Freed from manual labor, they applied themselves to metaphysical thought, abstract as an end in itself."[9] In addition to this freedom, they learned from their teacher Plato about the allegory of the cave, which, to this day in the social imaginary of Western cultures, privileges "pure" abstract ideas as true knowledge and disregards material things as deceptive appearances.

An example of how this ideology permeates the academy today is how the theological work that (mostly) Europeans and Euro-Americans produce lacking connection to experience, materiality, or bodies of flesh and bone is called "theology," but the theological work that (mostly) BIPOC (Black, Indigenous, and People of Color) persons produce, which is connected to their embodied experience and material conditions of their social locations, is called "contextual theology." The abundance of contextual theologies, scholarship in women's ways of knowing and being, and liberation theologies is not evidence against the academy privileging male ways of thinking and being. On the one hand, scholars that produce these works are expected to analyze and communicate in the same way that European men did before their arrival to "las Américas": through deductive abstract rational argumentation. On the other hand, if they deviate from said expectation, at worst, their work is classified as not "real" or "true" scholarship; at best, contextual theology is not as highly regarded as [insert here the undisclosed context] theology, in the same way that practical theology is not regarded as highly as [systematic or constructive] theology. In other words, all scholars, to be regarded as such, need to speak or write like those academics who learned from Plato to apply themselves to metaphysical, abstract thought as if they or we all come from the same social position.

That the academy is phallogocentric constitutes a problem in these times when nurturing diversity, equity, and inclusion is seemingly important to an institution's moral identity. Only valuing language of words in prose and deductive reasoning, the academy lacks resources to welcome and affirm the diversity of the students in their midst. Despite the presence of BIPOC, the academy still expects everyone to communicate in the same way. In addition, the academy is one of the cultural institutions ruling classes use to maintain power in a capitalist society. These are traditional moves of cultural hegemony and of colonization: those in power seek sameness by imposing their own ways as the standard.[10]

---

9. Eliseo Pérez Álvarez, *A voltear la tortilla: Método de la predicación anticolonialista* (Montevideo, Uruguay: Fundación Amerindia, 2020), 105. My translation.

10. See Antonio Gramsci's theory of cultural hegemony in his *Selections from the Prison*

Such is the academy into which I entered as a Puerto Rican cisgender heterosexual woman new to the United States, having lived a whole life speaking Spanish as my first language and residing in one of the few remaining colonies of the world. Both a US citizen and a foreigner in Nashville, Tennessee, there, in the belly of the empire, in the buckle of the bible belt, I devised and presented *Words & Flesh Entangled.*[11] The process of composing the play was similar to that of writing: make a mess and clean it up.[12] The origin of the knowledge is different though. It comes from the body rather than from abstract analysis.

When we presented *Words & Flesh Entangled* in 2018, it was not my intention to present the play as my thesis instead of a written dissertation.[13] I only needed to go through the creative process that I know best and communicate through one of my primary languages. Performing arts such as physical and experimental theater had become a primary language for me because I grew up in a church in which the pastor wrote plays all year long to present as sermons.[14] I had been in those plays since I was in the womb. I knew theater as a ritual and as a preaching language before I knew it as a means of cultural entertainment and later, as a pedagogy. I learned theater of the absurd and experimental theater at the University of Puerto Rico, Río Piedras campus, where I completed a Bachelor of Arts, secondary education, theatre major. I needed to conceive, grow, and birth *Words & Flesh Entangled* for myself, to feel alive, to keep alive my own traditions (which I did not find represented in the curriculum), and to help myself name, articulate, and translate my production of

---

Notebooks, ed. and trans. Quintin Hoare and Geoffrey Nowell-Smith (New York: International, 2008); and Frantz Fanon's *The Wretched of the Earth* (New York: Grove, 2004), with close attention to his notion of "colonized intellectual."

11. I do not capitalize the words "bible," "white," or "christian" because such conventions contribute to christian supremacy, which is closely tied to white supremacy, at least in the United States of America. The capital *B* commands respect for a book as if it should be sacred to everyone and not just christians. My choice of lower case intends to regard the bible as a collection of books, sacred for many people, especially for christians, and still accessible for interpretation through a variety of methods.

12. I am indebted to former English teacher, dream consultant, and spiritual director Laura Huff Hileman, who helped me to grow in the art of making a mess and cleaning it up.

13. I hired two professional actors, one to represent WORDS/FLESH and another to represent MM (the traditional though mistaken understanding of Mary Magdalene/muchas mujeres—*many women*). My gratitude to Diego Gómez and Veronica Dress. All the other characters were represented by members of the audience.

14. It was not a weekly practice, but it was more frequent than just twice a year for Easter and Christmas.

knowledge into the language that the academy required from me: English written words about abstract concepts organized in deductive argumentation.

Although it was not my intention to present the play as my thesis instead of a written dissertation, I certainly wished it. Now, over four years later, I write this essay in hopes that someday BIPOC may be allowed, invited even, to present their knowledge in their own languages, in their own communication patterns, with the affirmation from the academy that there are indeed multiple ways of knowing, of producing knowledge, and of sharing that knowledge.[15] For this hope to become a reality, we need a different academy. In that future academy that I imagine now, there is no phallogocentrism. Rather, that academy affirms Western, Eastern, Northern, and Southern hemispheric and global philosophical stances. That academy affirms a range of communication systems. That academy does not consider speech to be better than writing or vice versa, nor words to be better than bodily gestures. That academy values equally the phallic, the clitoral, and the intersex as part of symbolic orders. That academy honors and understands several epistemologies and several logics, including analytic, intellectual, cognitive, embodied, sexual, bodily, and performance logics, among others. That imagined academy is proficient in fleshly theopoetics.

15. The Conference on College Composition and Communication (CCCC) adopted in 1974 (reaffirmed in 2003 and 2014) a resolution on language that affirms "students' right to their own patterns and varieties of language—the dialects of their nurture or whatever dialects in which they find their own identity and style." For the whole resolution, see "Students' Right to Their Own Language," *College Composition and Communication* 25, no. 3, (Autumn, 1974): 1–18, https://cdn.ncte.org/nctefiles/groups/cccc/newsrtol.pdf. See Lisa Fink, "Students' Right to Their Own Language," *National Council of Teachers of English* (blog), March 19, 2015, https://ncte.org/blog/2015/03/students-right-to-their-own-language/. For the CCCC Statement on Second Language Writing and Multilingual Writers, Conferences on College Composition & Communication, "CCCC Statement on Second Language Writing and Multilingual Writers," last modified May 2020, https://cccc.ncte.org/cccc/resources/positions/secondlangwriting. While the resolution seeks to counter the myth of a standard American dialect, and not the use of English only, the resolution also aims to uplift and respect diverse heritage and cultural and racial diversity and to uphold students' right to their own language. In that same spirit, it is my hope that one day the resolution becomes a reality in all levels of the education system in the United States and that the desire to respect the heritage, culture, and right of the students to their own language be expanded to include other languages and systems of communication.

A Proposal for Fleshly Theopoetics

I consider *Words & Flesh Entangled* a work of fleshly theopoetics because it uses bodily expression rather than words. Due to phallogocentrism, the academy automatically thinks "poetry" when it hears "theopoetics." If we set aside the need for words and open up to the possibility of multiple means of expression, we can appreciate the theological *poiēsis* expressed in the play.

I understand fleshly theopoetics as making, remaking, and expressing theology through fleshly means, that is to say, in and through the materiality of bodies during the processes of generating theological knowledge and of communicating it. Drawing on the work of Amos Niven Wilder and Melanie A. Duguid-May, this section develops an understanding of fleshly theopoetics that (1) employs poetic language that is bodily and not necessarily poetic word; (2) honors imagination and the wisdom of the body; (3) names, although it is incomplete; and (4) mediates the nature of theological wisdom that words and rational logic cannot mediate.

The work of US American poet, tennis player, minister, and theology professor Amos Niven Wilder helps to develop the notion of poetic language that is not poetry. The work of US American poet, priest, and theology professor Melanie A. Duguid-May helps to explain the tasks that theopoetics plays in naming, remaining incomplete, and being appropriate given the nature of theology.

Poetic language encompasses more than poetry. In *Theopoetic: Theology and the Religious Imagination*, Wilder had already created space for multiple genres to produce theopoetics when in 1976 he acknowledged poetic languages other than poetry. In his elaboration of a theopoetic, Wilder provides examples of several arts that were changing or emerging and reflecting cultural changes in perception and consciousness. His examples include theater of the absurd, the *noveau roman*, fictions, abstract impressionism, projective verse, fantasy and the psychedelic, avant-garde theatre, graphic arts, architecture, stained glass, hymns, religious drama, performing arts, and multimedia presentations.[16] Wilder also points out that challenging the myth of objective consciousness or rationalism manifests in "a return to spontaneity, imagination, the wisdom of the body, cosmic rhythms, and uninhibited immediacy of awareness."[17]

---

16. Amos N. Wilder, *Theopoetic: Theology and the Religious Imagination* (Philadelphia: Fortress, 1976), 30–31, and 44, 53, 55.

17. Wilder, *Theopoetic*, 31.

Words & Flesh Entangled generates theological reflection through suitable languages. The play is a work of performing arts such as physical and experimental theater. According to Wilder's theopoetic, performing arts employ suitable poetic languages to generate theological reflection. In addition, the play constitutes a distinct doctoral thesis that is out of place and out of context. Doctoral theses in the Graduate Department of Religion of Vanderbilt University are typically presented and defended in a classroom or conference room using logical prose; they are neither physical nor experimental theater, and they are not shared in a chapel. The choices of venue and language challenge the myth of objective consciousness and emphasize imagination and the wisdom of the body. Wilder's work on theopoetics offers the possibility to affirm that *Words & Flesh Entangled* is fleshly theopoetics in bodily language, performed poetry without words.

Theopoetics engages in naming, is often incomplete, yet is necessary given the nature of theological wisdom. In *A Body Knows: A Theopoetics of Death and Resurrection*, May categorizes her own work as theopoetics based on three reasons: naming, incompletion, and the nature of theological wisdom. First, she draws on the works of Wilder and Audre Lorde to establish that poetry helps to name something so the thing named can be thought. In this sense, poetry is a bridge.

Second, May draws on the work of Christine Downing's emphasis on making. May quotes from Downing, "A *poesis* [*sic*], means seeing it as always still in the process of being made and remade."[18] May's rephrasing of the concept is that a *poiēsis* is an "ongoing process of naming, clarifying, and loosing again: to honor *poesis* [*sic*] as making and remaking without ceasing."[19] For May, this process implies introducing alternative or new perspectives that "are not conceptually complete or systematically settled."[20] The phrase "alternative perspectives" resonates with alternative methods for theologizing: alternative interpretations, alternative roads, alternative versions of theology, what Argentinian theologian Marcella Althaus-Reid calls "per/versions."[21] Conceptual incompleteness, unsettledness, and alternatives point to the inconclusive unconventional nature of theopoetics. In the words of US minister and professor of contextual education Callid Keefe-Perry, theopoetics is "an acceptance of cognitive uncertainty regarding the Divine."[22] Keefe-Perry adds that with ac-

---

18. Melanie A. May, *A Body Knows: A Theopoetics of Death and Resurrection* (New York: Continuum, 1995), 24.

19. May, *A Body Knows*, 25.

20. May, *A Body Knows*, 25.

21. See Marcella Althaus-Reid, *Indecent Theology: Theological Perversions in Sex, Gender and Politics* (London: Routledge, 2001).

22. L. Callid Keefe-Perry, *Way to Water: A Theopoetics Primer* (Eugene, OR: Cascade Books, 2014), 130, Kindle.

ceptance comes the indisposition to unjustifiably eliminate that uncertainty. Fleshly theopoetics makes incomplete per/versions that accept and show uncertainty regarding the Divine.

Third, inspired by and in the company of poet Saint Ephrem of fourth-century Syria, May affirms that there is theological wisdom that cannot be conveyed except through poetic pronunciation.[23] Theological wisdom is mystery, ambiguity that has more aspects than those for which reason can account. Consequently, theopoetics turns to "action and creative articulation."[24] Theopoetics turns to poetic language to communicate what words in prose cannot communicate about theological wisdom.

Generating the play *Words & Flesh Entangled* served the purpose for me of bridging embodied knowledge and analytic thought through naming.[25] I sought bodily wisdom that would help me articulate in academic scholastic jargon and words what my body already knew. In other words, I must perform it to be able to explain it, if it can be explained at all. To Wilder's words "Before the message there must be the vision, before the sermon the hymn, before the prose the poem,"[26] I add, "before the dissertation, the bodily performance." *Words & Flesh Entangled* is theopoetics because, in May's words, it helps "give name to the nameless so it can be thought."[27]

In addition to naming, the presentation of the play *Words & Flesh Entangled* lives into incompletion in various ways. First, to be performed, it requires volunteers from the audience. Second, it abstains from words in such a way that invites the spect-actors to participate, to ascribe meaning to the movements, stillness, and symbols in the performance. Third, at the end of the play the character WORDS/FLESH is still processing the discovery of the rainbow that exists between words and flesh. There is no conclusion in the journey of that character. Fourth, the eucharistic picnic and the circle around it are incomplete and require the participation of the spect-actors. Per May's work, the play is theopoetics because it is incomplete and alternative.

Words & Flesh Entangled also demonstrates the nature of theological wisdom as one that needs poetic articulation. There are aspects of preaching and of being a preacher that are best shown through poetic performing arts than through

23. May, *A Body Knows*, 25.

24. Keefe-Perry, *Way to Water*, 111.

25. Per the brief description of the play offered above, the reader may already notice that bodily wisdom in the play *Words & Flesh Entangled* names struggle between words and flesh and an inseparability between them.

26. Wilder, *Theopoetic*, 1.

27. May, *A Body Knows*, 24. Here, May quotes Audre Lorde, "Poetry Is Not a Luxury," in *Sister Outsider: Essays and Speeches by Audre Lorde* (Freedom, CA: Crossing, 1984), 37.

logical prose. These are the aspects that the play addresses in its content. Silent bodily performing art demonstrates and defies how preaching is also phallogocentric in a way that carefully crafted written words cannot. There are aspects of scholarship, understood as the production of knowledge, and of being a scholar of color that are best shown through poetic performing arts than through logical prose. These are the aspects that the play addresses in its form, in its choice to be a work of fleshly theopoetics rather than pages full of words. It does not make much sense, at least to me, to challenge phallogocentrism through phallogocentric means. Thus, it was necessary to get help from silence and flesh, from bodily movement and stillness, in sum, from fleshly theopoetics to challenge phallogocentrism both in preaching and in the scholarly production of homiletics.

This proposal for fleshly theopoetics is distinct from poetics of the flesh. A seemingly inverted process calls for an inversion of terms. Let me explain. In *Poetics of the Flesh*, Puerto Rican theologian and professor of religion and Latinx studies Mayra Rivera proposes that poetics of the flesh deploys negations (or apophatic gestures) of multiplication to counter reifications of ancient imaginaries of "body" and "flesh."[28] To make her argument, Rivera draws in part from Caribbean poets and demonstrates how their poetry reflects the materiality of their lives. The knowledge that these poets share in beautiful words comes from their embodied experience. The Caribbean poets Rivera engages, May's self-crafted theopoetics, and my voice in this essay employ a process that begins first in embodied experience then follows up with intellectual reflection and analysis (or not) producing words; this can be poetry or prose. We are writing from the body.

Words & Flesh Entangled was not produced in such a way. Rather, in good experimental fashion as I learned from Puerto Rican theater artist and pedagogue Rosa Luisa Márquez, I produced the play bracketing cognition and reason, thinking bodily, listening to and manifesting embodied wisdom, letting the body be, do, and communicate. For those reasons, some may think the process used to generate the play is backward or the inverse of what should be.

Assuming that art is a mode of expression that "embellishes" an abstract yet carefully crafted idea, a person may think that *Words & Flesh Entangled* "translates" into theatrics or performing arts. To them my dissertation thesis is, in a way, similar to the writing of Caribbean poetry that Rivera uplifts, or a theopoetics of death and resurrection that May develops, or an essay about fleshly theopoetics like this one. I do not agree with such an assumption. From the perspective of a life-long theater maker who specialized in experimental theater and a scholar, I contend that the opposite is true and is not true.

28. Mayra Rivera, *Poetics of the Flesh* (Durham, NC: Duke University Press, 2015).

The opposite is true because in the case of the play *Words & Flesh Entangled,* instead of "translating" into performing art a previous abstract yet carefully crafted idea, I let our bodies (mine and those of the actors) do the thinking first.[29] This kind of bodily thinking happens when the body performs what it wants, not what a thinking mind that has reflected on a prior embodied experience tells the body to perform. Art is not a mode of expression that "embellishes" an abstract yet carefully crafted idea. Art expresses. Art generates ideas. *Words & Flesh Entangled* did not translate ideas into theatrics or performing arts. The play facilitated the generation of ideas from and through bodies.

It was only later that I attempted to "translate" some ideas from performing arts to scholarly words that took the shape of a doctoral written dissertation. It was through later reflection that I "translated" into carefully crafted words a prior artistically crafted embodied idea, as I do in writing this essay. In such a way, I lived into the aforementioned assumption of artistic embellishment of an abstract idea and its possible "translation."[30] The "translation" was not from abstract ideas to embellishment or art; just the opposite. The "translation" went from art to ideas and words. Some concepts of the play made it into the final

29. Mayra Rivera has written about thinking bodies, but not in the way that I mean here. In Rivera's essay, thinking bodies are those that write body-words out of their embodied experience. Rivera offers as examples Marcella Althaus-Reid, who kept the body at the center of her theology, *mujerista* theology as Ada María Isasi-Díaz developed it out of the embodied experience of Latinas living in the United States, and songs and poems. All of those works, like this essay, emerge from the corporeality of bodies, from embodied experiences, and at the end produce words, whether in poetry or prose. The kind of thinking that I mean here is the one that Tito and Rosa Luisa taught me in the theater department of the University of Puerto Rico when in the course *Brincos y Saltos* they invited us to stop thinking and let the bodies express themselves. It is the kind of thinking with the body that doing sculpture work requires, as when I facilitate theater of the oppressed workshops. When doing sculptures with your body as clay, do not think, just react bodily because your body knows, and if you think, you will probably censor your body. Even if you do not censor your body, you might be sculpting what you consciously know but not what your body knows. Mayra Rivera, "Thinking Bodies: The Spirit of a Latina Incarnational Imagination," in *Decolonizing Epistemologies: Latina/o Theology and Philosophy*, ed. Ada María Isasi-Díaz and Eduardo Mendieta (New York: Fordham University Press, 2012), 207–25.

30. I find the word "embellishment" to be a subtle (not so subtle) way to disregard and belittle the work of "artists" as less than the work of philosophers. I use it here because during the process of developing my dissertation, I heard it in regard to my performing art. I also heard the assumption that I discuss in this paragraph. About the impossibility of translating performances or performing works of art, see Diana Taylor, "Denise Stoklos: The Politics of Decipherability," in *The Archive and the Repertoire: Performing Cultural Memory in the Americas* (Durham, NC: Duke University Press, 2003), 212–36.

written dissertation. The reality is that *Words & Flesh Entangled* communicates something and my written dissertation communicates something else, which takes us to why the opposite of the initial assumption is not true.

The opposite is not true because the bodily utterances in the play *Words & Flesh Entangled* were not a translation but a claim on itself that began, was processed, composed, polished, and presented from the body and through bodily means of communication. In other words, fleshly theopoetics is sort of the opposite of poetics of the flesh. Fleshly theopoetics is not poetry that arises from bodily experience. It is bodily poetry that creates an experience. This is so because fleshly theopoetics is also a way of knowing, a system of knowledge and expression in which the flesh in embodied action, in performance, is the episteme.[31] The flesh is the knower and the means. The flesh communicates for itself rather than mediates the communication of another aspect of the being. Rivera's *Poetics of the Flesh* and my *Fleshly Theopoetics* side by side announce that there is (or could be, maybe even ought to be) space in the academy for both approaches.

To summarize, this essay proposes that fleshly theopoetics is theological *poiēsis,* an ongoing process of making, remaking, and expressing theology through the materiality of bodies during the processes of generating and of communicating theological knowledge. Fleshly theopoetics employs poetic language that is bodily and does not necessarily use words, honors imagination and the wisdom of the body, names, is incomplete per/version, and mediates the mysterious and ambiguous nature of theological wisdom. Fleshly theopoetics, like poetics of the flesh, emerges from the body, but unlike poetics of the flesh, it grows and produces fleshly communication, not words, not poems, not songs, not prose, but rather artistic performance.

IMPLICATIONS, APPLICATIONS, AND INVITATIONS FROM FLESHLY THEOPOETICS

The prior proposal for the acceptance of fleshly theopoetics implies that it is a language in its own right that perhaps one day will be accepted in the academy. In addition, fleshly theopoetics is capable of generating a range of genres or utterances for different purposes with different messaging. While fleshly theopoetics is not for everyone, its consideration as an autochthonous (or indigenous) and valid language for some groups in some contexts invites all bodies to make and communicate theological knowledge through their autochthonous and best languages.

31. About performance as an episteme, see in general, Taylor, *Archive and the Repertoire.*

Fleshly theopoetics is a language in its own right; it is a communication system suitable to express prayers, sermons, and arguments, as well as suitable to make theology. If words are used to form a wide range of genres, what prohibits flesh from doing the same? This essay focuses on phallogocentrism as opposition to fleshly theopoetics. Once we realize that phallogocentrism obfuscates our perceptions and willingness to listen, we can be open to the possibility of fleshly theopoetics being an acceptable language for the production of knowledge in the academy.

Dislodging phallogocentrism results in perceiving how flesh is also capable of generating a wide range of genres. Better yet, flesh can accomplish many goals. Flesh can instruct, delight, pray, preach, teach, argue, protest, transgress, move its audience, challenge the status quo, and introduce alternative futures. Which genre the flesh is producing depends on the content and context. For example, if addressing the Divine in praise for what the Divine is and has done in the midst of a liturgy, the flesh is producing a prayer. If addressing a congregation, sharing an interpretation of a sacred text, whether from the pulpit in a worship service or from the sidewalk across the street from the church building, the flesh is producing a sermon. If addressing scholars or classmates, sharing knowledge new to the sender and/or receiver of communication, the flesh is producing academic knowledge. Content and context help audiences identify what genre fleshly theopoetics is generating.

Fleshly theopoetics is not for everyone, but then again, neither is oration or writing in prose. In fact, I have been implicitly stating that this essay's invitation to generate fleshly theopoetics is for BIPOC, even though I know that there are people who are not BIPOC who communicate or even do and make theology through performing or other kinds of "arts."[32] The invitation to generate fleshly theopoetics is for those who have the natural or acquired skills, who feel called to use this communication system or who live among a community that understands this language because they use it frequently.

Even those who know and use the language of the flesh to communicate need to exercise wisdom as to when, for what reason, and before whom to do it. Not all places and communities welcome or understand fleshly theopoetics. Nonetheless, the goal of communication is not always clarity and understanding. Fleshly theopoetics out of place and time may transgress, may challenge

---

32. I use quotation marks around the word "arts" to convey that the label reflects a certain worldview. The more I learn about performance studies (here, I am not referring to performing arts), the less I agree that theater, music, painting, dance, visual representation, architecture, poetry, and film are arts and the more I think they are communication systems that are or were perceived differently in other times, spaces, and cultures.

the status quo and introduce alternatives and possibilities. Fleshly theopoetics may also serve as a way for the theopoet, that is, the practitioner of theopoetics, to speak their own language or to stay or feel alive. This was the case for me when I devised and presented *Words & Flesh Entangled*.

Even though the invitation to generate fleshly theopoetics is not for everyone, there is an invitation for everyone in this essay. Drawing on my embodied experience of performing fleshly theopoetics for the academy and for the church, I invite every single and communal body to express themselves in their autochthonous and best languages.

In Conclusion

Fleshly theopoetics is embodied knowledge making theology through embodied performance. Flesh itself gestates and gives birth to theological knowledge. There is no flawless translation into poetry or words. There is so much more to say about fleshly theopoetics. These pages constitute only a teaser, a taste of what fleshly theopoetics can be if only we are willing to hear and see.

Works Cited

Althaus-Reid, Marcella. *Indecent Theology: Theological Perversions in Sex, Gender and Politics*. London: Routledge, 2001.

Aredez, Carmina. "El teatro realista y Sus características más destacadas." Espectáculos BCN, September 21, 2020. https://www.espectaculosbcn.com /teatro-realista-caracteristicas/.

Boal, Augusto. *Theatre of the Oppressed*. Translated by Charles A. and Maria-Odilia Leal McBride. New York: Theatre Communications, 1985.

Conference on College and Composition. "Students' Right to Their Own Language." *College Composition and Communication* 25, no. 3 (Autumn, 1974): 1–18. https://cdn.ncte.org/nctefiles/groups/cccc/newsrtol.pdf.

Conference on College Composition & Communication. "CCCC Statement on Second Language Writing and Multilingual Writers." Last modified May 2020. https://cccc.ncte.org/cccc/resources/positions/secondlangwriting.

D'Urso, Agustina, and Jason H. Brickner. "Mechanisms of Epigenetic Memory." *Trends in Genetics* 30, no. 6 (June 2014): 230–36.

Fanon, Frantz. *The Wretched of the Earth*. New York: Grove, 2004.

Fink, Lisa. "Students' Right to Their Own Language." *National Council of Teach-*

ers of English (blog). March 19, 2015. https://ncte.org/blog/2015/03/students-right-to-their-own-language/.

Gramsci, Antonio. *Selections from the Prison Notebooks.* Edited and translated by Quintin Hoare and Geoffrey Nowell-Smith. New York: International, 2008.

Innes, Christopher. *Avant Garde Theatre: 1892–1992.* London: Routledge, 1993.

Keefe-Perry, L. Callid. *Way to Water: A Theopoetics Primer.* Eugene, OR: Cascade, 2014. Kindle.

Klages, Mary. *Literary Theory: The Complete Guide.* London: Bloomsbury Academic, 2017. Kindle.

Lorde, Audre. "Poetry Is Not a Luxury." In *Sister Outsider: Essays and Speeches by Audre Lorde*, 37. Freedom, CA: Crossing, 1984.

Márquez, Rosa Luisa. *Brincos y saltos: El juego como disciplina teatral; Ensayos y manual de teatreros ambulantes.* Cayey, PR: Ediciones Cuicaloca con el Co-auspicio del Colegio Universitario de Cayey, 1992.

May, Melanie A. *A Body Knows: A Theopoetics of Death and Resurrection.* New York: Continuum, 1995.

Pérez Álvarez, Eliseo. *A voltear la tortilla: Método de la predicación anticolonialista.* Montevideo, Uruguay: Fundación Amerindia, 2020.

Rivera, Mayra. *Poetics of the Flesh.* Durham, NC: Duke University Press, 2015.

———. "Thinking Bodies: The Spirit of a Latina Incarnational Imagination." In *Decolonizing Epistemologies: Latina/o Theology and Philosophy*, edited by Ada María Isasi-Díaz and Eduardo Mendieta, 207–25. New York: Fordham University Press, 2012.

Schirle, Joan. "Potholes in the Road to Devising." *Theatre Topics* 15, no. 1 (March 2005): 91–102.

Stephens, Tim. "Study Shows How Epigenetic Memory Is Passed across Generations." *UC Santa Cruz News*, September 18, 2014. https://news.ucsc.edu/2014/09/epigenetics.html.

Taylor, Diana. *The Archive and the Repertoire: Performing Cultural Memory in the Americas.* Durham, NC: Duke University Press, 2003.

———. "Denise Stoklos: The Politics of Decipherability." In *Archive and the Repertoire*, 212–36.

Tran, Diep. "What Is Physical Theater?" *Backstage Magazine.* Last updated April 18, 2022. https://www.backstage.com/magazine/article/physical-theater-guide-74965/.

Wilder, Amos N. *Theopoetic: Theology and the Religious Imagination.* Philadelphia: Fortress, 1976.

3

Toward a Theopoetic Wholeness

A Womanist Reflection in the Theological Academy

LAKISHA R. LOCKHART-RUSCH

After about two months of working on my dissertation, I had a meeting with a professor to discuss a chapter and things to improve (I was incredibly nervous, yet excited).

SCENE:

PROF.: Good morning.

LL: Good morning!

PROF.: All right, let's jump in. So, it's good . . . it's just the way you write.

LL: The way I write? (The way I write? I wrote like I was trained to write . . . is it that bad?)

PROF.: Yes. It's so verbose and complicated. Just say what you want to say.

LL: OK, can you be more specific? I thought that is what I was doing, while also being sure to use particular religious jargon. Was it too much? (Is he saying that I'm using too many big words? Is it because I am centering Black and Brown voices? I am using all the great scholars, just like I was trained to do).

PROF.: Yes.

LL: OK, what would you suggest? (Tell me something, I just wanna write this and be done!)

PROF.: Just . . . well . . . just write more "Anglo-Saxon."

LL: I'm sorry, what? (WHAT IN THE WHOLE HELL???? I know I didn't hear that right . . . I must have misheard.)

PROF.: You know, write more "Anglo-Saxon" so people can understand.

LL: OK, well I don't identify as Anglo-Saxon so it will be difficult for me to write in that manner. (What the hell? What kind of thing is that to say to a Black woman who is literally writing about womanism with Black and Brown theologians? Seriously?! And I still have no idea what it means to write this way because I am not White.
Is he serious?

I literally cannot breathe right now!
What am I going to do?
How will I finish this dissertation?
Will I finish?
Clearly my writing and my work are not good enough.
How did I even get into this program?)

Fast forward three months to a time when I was finally able to let go of this narrative. This exchange tore me apart—to pieces. I could literally not write anything for months because I kept questioning everything I wrote. I would write and then delete, write and delete, write and delete . . . delete . . . delete. Internally I was a mess, my body and my mind were literally at odds. My mind knew the literature and what to write, but my body did too. My body wanted me to write in my voice, my style, a way that felt more like me, but my mind kept telling me that clearly my voice was not good enough because it was not "Anglo-Saxon" enough.

At the suggestion of another professor (a Black woman) I began writing two dissertations, one for me and my body and another for my professor and my mind. (Talk about not being whole—this was a nightmare). While it was difficult to do this, it gave me enough space to finish. I was able to appease both parts of me as well as my professor, and I was able to finish. However, it was far from a wholistic or wholesome experience and I was far from whole.

Wholistic . . .
Wholesome . . .
Whole . . .
. . . HOLE

The theological academy has a responsibility toward student's spiritual growth and evolution or, as we often call it, spiritual formation. What if everyone could be whole in the theological academy? I mean genuinely whole in body, mind, and spirit. What would that take? Where would we start? What would that even look like? In this chapter, I would like to do something I do not get to do very often, which is to dream. For me, the act of dreaming is resistance, and I believe to be more whole we have to do things differently and resist the many ways the academy picks away at the pieces of who we are through inhumane expectations of constant production with little to no care for the actual person. I would like to dream of what could be if we were all whole and practiced a more theopoetic wholeness, where a person's body, mind, and spirit are valued and cared for in both the expression of their life and work in the theological academy. A wholeness that takes seriously the form, style, and as Dr. Oredein states in the introduction of this book, the "expression of life in process," which includes the body. Come dream with me for a moment of a theological academy that is moving toward a more theopoetic wholeness.

Essential Understandings

The scene I laid out in the introduction is mild considering other things I have heard from other colleagues and friends of color in the theological academy (which are atrocious). However, this is where Dr. Emilie Townes' fantastic hegemonic imagination comes into play.[1] The fantastic hegemonic imagination allows for the dominant culture and narrative to continue these and other acts of violence on and toward Black, Brown, and different bodies (you know what different bodies are—queer bodies, trans bodies, differently abled bodies, neurodivergent bodies . . .). This "diseased imagination"[2] allows those in power to continue to think and act superior as they see anyone who is not them or like them and treat them as inferior. This continues to live and breathe in the halls of the academy today (I dare you to tell someone about your story. . . . I know you have one).

The very structure, form, and style of the academy is oppressive. After all, it was originally meant solely for White, able-bodied, cishetero men with a certain economic status. Over the years all the theological academy has really done is keep that same colonized structure, form, and style, while periodically allowing other bodies to enter. Other bodies that these walls, spaces, style, and form were not made for. Many academic spaces do not embody an ethos of

---

1. Emilie Townes, *Womanist Ethics and the Cultural Production of Evil* (New York: Palgrave Macmillan, 2006), 21.

2. Willie James Jennings, *The Christian Imagination* (New Haven: Yale University Press, 2010), 8.

welcome or human dignity and care. How can institutions care for the person when they are too busy worrying about "profit to be prophetic"?[3] What is often the most egregious is being in the area of religious education at seminaries and institutions that claim a faith and belief in the human dignity of all yet remain oppressive and inhuman in practice. How is one to survive (not even thrive . . . just make it) when one is not able to bring one's whole embodied self into the classroom space?

However, I continue to have hope. I must, for my students, for my children, and for myself. It is with this hope in mind that I invite you to dream with me of a more equitable, decolonized, humane academy. One that is moving toward a more theopoetic wholeness as it reframes what teaching and learning can mean and look like, makes space to support faculty, and dismantles the notion of isolation and silos for a more collaborative and embodied approach that can leave all of us more whole.

TEACHING AND LEARNING

What if the academy was a place that not only respected and supported the many ways scholars show up but also provided space and opportunity for scholars to continue to live into that wholeness. Let's dream for a moment of practicing a more whole theopoetic within the academy in two ways: through embedding creative and equitable practices in teaching and learning, and re-imagining sabbaticals and the tenure and promotion process.

I dream of an academy that values creativity and equity not just in talk but in practice. What this looks like is not only allowing educators and theologians space to be as creative and innovative as they like with their classes but normalizing such pedagogical imagination. This can look like making space for class outside and allowing for more creative assignments and rubrics rather than written assignments alone. It means taking seriously different bodies with various epistemological pathways and offering various modalities of participation like poetry, Prezi, Canva, photography, songs, voice threads, videos, comics, LEGO, Play-Doh, and so many more options. It means taking seriously multiple intelligences and neurodivergence. What if, instead of another written essay about one's theological understanding, students were able to create a storyboard or a comic book? Not only would that be much more exciting to

---

3. Lakisha Lockhart, "My Wildest Dream: A Letter to My Black Son," *Religious Education Journal* 115, no. 1 (January 2020): 92–99.

grade (I love grading these assignments and really getting to know students), but imagine how much more is internalized and experienced by the students when they are able to express themselves in a way that feels more like them? To have their way of being and making meaning of the divine valued and appreciated is to see God reflected in themselves, and that is not only important; it is transformative and liberating.

I dream of an academy where we can actively resist the colonized structure and grading system through the act of ungrading. Ungrading takes the grading out of the process of evaluating students. Ungrading "gives purpose to feedback by offering a learning environment where students can take risks, fail and improve upon their work. Ungrading is a classroom paradigm shift that places the focus of education back on what is being learned and why, rather than what is being produced and for whom."[4] I cannot tell you the number of times students have been diminished by a grade thinking this is all they are worth (it's me . . . I am students). We are so much more than a letter grade, especially when the person giving that grade does not understand the many ways people come to know and understand the divine in relation to their work. I have started using ungrading for about the last few years in my classes, and it has been a liberating experience for both myself as an educator and my students.

I let my students know that I will be using the ungrading technique to measure their progress the very first day. I let them know that they will never get a letter grade on any assignment from me—just feedback, conversation, and questions to reflect on and go deeper. I make personal notes of participation, group work, and assignments along the way. Then at the end of the class I have them complete a self-evaluation about the course, what they did, and how they would grade themselves. I match my notes with their evaluation, and if we are in sync, the grade they suggested stands. If they do not match, I have a conversation with the student, and we come to a grade together. I have noticed that negotiating mismatched grades usually happens mostly with women, especially women of color, as they are often much harder on themselves because of the message the world continuously sends them. I find myself pulling out receipts (always keep your receipts . . . always). I show them where they have gone above and beyond the work asked and how they need to value their contributions and show themself the same grace they show everyone else. Through my experience with ungrading, I have not only been able to provide more equity in my class, but also my students have been able to engage

---

4. "Ungrading," Baylor University, Academy for Teaching and Learning, https://www.baylor.edu/atl/index.php?id=984862.

deeply in coursework without the constant is-this-what-the-professor-wants anxiety narrative in the back of their minds. Several student evaluations have mentioned how one of my classes was the first time they did not have to worry about a grade; this freed them up to be more creative, truly present, and in the moment. One student said his faith finally felt free for the first time in seminary (he was in his final semester). This is the kind of embodied theopoetic wholeness I want for all my students. Furthermore, as a professor, not having to offer a grade on everything is incredibly freeing as well. It allows me to be a better and more engaged educator. I can try more creative and innovative practices that make a difference for my students and for me.

My next bit of dreaming might be very contentious. I want to dream of a reimagined sabbatical and tenure and promotion process. Let's start with sabbatical. For those not familiar with sabbatical, it is basically a time after a certain number of years of work at the institution that faculty are able to request off from teaching and committee duties with the expectation that upon their return they would have produced a scholarly contribution to the field (i.e., they would have worked on a book, presented at a conference, written some chapters, or generated something as a result of lots of production and work and little rest). This is the problem. What if institutions, especially our religious institutions, leaned further into the "sabbath" of sabbatical and allowed scholars a place of genuine rest, rejuvenation, and re-centering instead of further demands of production. (I know this is a lot to ask, but hey this is my dream!) I wonder how much more generative a sabbatical would be if contribution to self was valued more than contribution to the field. Don't get me wrong, if folks want to use that time to write and research, they are welcome to, but it should be a choice, not a demand. Studies show that people are 20 percent more productive in their work after they have had time for genuine rest, play, and recreation.[5] I wonder how much institutions would be made better with faculty who have time for rest and play. I wonder what new classes could be created, what new perspectives could emerge, and what kind of ethos and collaboration might be made possible when centering everyone's wholeness, not just in word and theory but in real institutional practice?

What if our tenure and promotion process considered the whole person, especially in how one's personal wellness impacts their pedagogy? What if, along

5. Mark J. Keith, Greg Anderson, James Gaskin, and Douglas L. Dean, "Team Video Gaming for Team Building: Effects on Team Performance," *AIS Transactions on Human-Computer Interaction* 10, no. 4 (December 31, 2018): 205–31, https://doi.org/DOI: 10.17705/1thci.00110.

with contribution to the field, contribution to community and publications, there was also space for creative endeavors that impacted one's personhood and teaching, like being involved in Godly play or theater of the oppressed, taking up photography, or doing a cooking challenge? What if there was also a space for personal wellness through therapy, hiking, and or playing with the two little humans you are keeping alive and well (speaking of the self . . .). We bring all of who we are to the institutions in which we teach, and our teaching is affected by all our experiences. I am a better educator because I am a mother. I am a better educator because I play. My classrooms are made better not just because of my publications but because of the very essence of who I am and what I experience in my body daily. What if tenure and promotion took that seriously and considered all of someone, not just pieces and parts?

I will end this section with a less contentious idea of collaboration. I will put it plainly and simply: we are made better together. The theological academy is often very isolating, with folks in many areas often staying within their areas and not branching out to work with other scholars in other departmental areas or theological disciplines. What if we stopped the departmental isolation and disciplinary siloing? What if Bible and Christian education departments worked together to create a course and co-taught it? What if faculty collaborated not only across departments but also across institutions? So many of us are actually friends who use each other's work on a regular basis, so why not do more collaborating? With technology we can do more class sharing, guest facilitating, and group conversations. Why not take advantage of that? I will say this again: we are better together.

Physical Space

I want institutions to take inventory of who is in your space. What do you see? What are the ages? What are the racial and ethnic makeups? What and where are the religious beliefs? What are the sexual identities? What are the gender identities? What are the various abilities and disabilities (both visual and non-visual)? Write it, draw it, take a picture . . . capture it in some way.

Now look around your room, your space. Is your space welcoming to all that you named? Would a wheelchair-bound person be able to enter the space without hassle? Would a transgender person be able to use the restroom without hassle? Do they see themselves reflected in this space? Is it theirs?

What might need to change or shift for your space to reflect those that are within it?

What if institutions did this exercise? I believe many would find that their physical spaces were created and still are made for White able-bodied cis-hetero men. I get it, you cannot do away with these precious structures that cost a fortune and need to be used. However, you can alter them to be more and do more to represent the whole of who you employ and educate. You can put in ramps, put proper signage on restrooms, ensure that classrooms and offices have windows, and have more diverse artwork on the walls. Value these realities not just in theory but also in practice through a strategic plan and a budget with implementation phases.

What if along with classrooms, offices, and break rooms institutions had parenting lounges for professors, staff, and students who might be nursing or feeding a child and need a private space. (This was me. Having to breastfeed— yes, I said "breast" in an academic book chapter—in my office with beautiful windows was a horrible experience for me and my baby.) What if there was a designated space for nursing with a fridge, tape, and sharpies for labeling—a place that would care for the whole person in various walks of life? (I would also advocate for childcare, but I know that is really stretching things.)

What if institutions had relax/meditation/play rooms or spaces throughout campus? Places with blankets and pillows to use when needed, with snacks and beverages and games to enjoy, with meditation rugs and low lighting to take advantage of when needed. The academy can be an exhausting, isolating, and overstimulating place for some, so offering space for students, staff, and faculty to re-center themselves and get their needs met is a way of offering a more whole theopoetic in practice.

Conclusion

It is nice to dream of a theopoetic of wholeness where the form, style, language, and art of being whole are valued and seen as an integral part of what it means to be human in the academy (such a beautiful dream!). And also, what if we could make it a reality? What if we could flourish instead of just survive? What if we held institutions accountable to their mission statements and strategic plans they love to bring out during meetings and display on websites? The pursuit of a theopoetic wholeness in the theological academy fulfills mission statues, strategic plans, and value statements. What if we held those boundaries? While it is a beautiful dream, what if it was a reality? What if we chose ungrading in our classrooms to resist the Eurocentric and colonial grading system to provide our students with a more wholistic class experience? What if we chose to include keeping two tiny humans alive and well in our tenure and promotion portfolios? What if we chose to not meet in offices or classrooms with no windows? What if we are the ones to make these dreams reality? What if we are the ones to change the narrative, paint a different picture, change the channel, play another song, or write another book? What if we are the ones who do not have to dream because we are already awake? What if we are the ones to really push ourselves toward living out a more wholesome theopoetic? (Yes, I'm talking about you.) Let's do more than dream together . . . let's be whole together.

> Hole . . .
> Wholesome . . .
> Wholistic . . .
> WHOLE!

Works Cited

Jennings, Willie James. *The Christian Imagination: Theology and the Origins of Race*. New Haven: Yale University Press, 2010.

Keith, Mark J., Greg Anderson, James Gaskin, and Douglas L. Dean. "Team Video Gaming for Team Building: Effects on Team Performance." *AIS Transactions on Human-Computer Interaction* 10, no. 4 (December 31, 2018): 205–31. https://doi.org/DOI: 10.17705/1thci.00110.

Lockhart, Lakisha. "My Wildest Dream: A Letter to My Black Son." *Religious Education Journal* 115, no. 1 (January 2020): 92–99.

Townes, Emilie. *Womanist Ethics and the Cultural Production of Evil*. New York: Palgrave Macmillan, 2006.

"Ungrading." Baylor University, Academy for Teaching and Learning. https://www.baylor.edu/atl/index.php?id=984862.

Part 2

Methods and Inquiries

4

Listening Theopoetically

Methods and Approaches for Researching with a Theopoetic Ear

TIFFANY U. TRENT

When we moved to a new city in my high school years, the first thing my mother did was start looking for a church home. Each week, two of my sisters and I paid attention to the singing, to the Sunday School and youth group options, plus whether any new friends we had met were part of the congregation. My youngest sister, however, coming into awareness as a sixth grader of the intellectual depth she would prove to have, applied an additional assessment. She employed the unary numeral system of "tally marks" on her church bulletin to document the quality and preparation of the sermons by counting how many times the preacher said "um." Needless to say, at one service, as her tallying spanned multiple pages of the whitespace in the bulletin, even the older three of us were on the verge of embarrassing our mother in our new environment. The child's penchant for computation was funny . . . and inappropriate . . . and was—and still is!—her gift.

Yet, some twenty years later, a seminary classmate's "mm" and "hmm" in the course *History of Christian Thought* was my cue that the professor was preaching as well as teaching; my classmate's "mm-hmm" cued me that there were deeper codes for me to analyze in my notes. This peer, who was already a pastor, was a barometer for me of depths that I thought I did not understand yet but could learn from. If he said "mm" as if he was listening to good preaching, there was something else happening in addition to the historical data that the instructor was reporting. In a context where students would ask, "How can I say this from the pulpit?" my classmate was a data source that

a. I chose to value (through theopoetic listening),
b. I trusted had done some analysis, and
c. I had faith (confidence) could do meaningful and relevant analysis.

B and C are indeed different. Whether my classmate had already made the leap from historical Christianity to the current preaching moment or whether he was inspired to work toward that are different efforts. Beloved, I propose that theopoetic listening enlivens exegeting the data. *I define theopoetic listening as a methodology that invokes and heeds call and response, interimagining between body(ies) and spirit to witness the holy.* In these days of acknowledging bias in ourselves, in our AI, and our ostensibly objective algorithms, in addition to the scholarly gains that result from transparency about the researcher's social location and lens, listening theopoetically benefits qualitative research design, coding choices, and data analysis *for the questions I care to ask.*

I am a Gen-X Black woman, theater director, teacher, minister. I was raised mid-Atlantic, South, and Midwest. I like regionalisms. I like Black and African American regionalisms: how we do food, how we do church, how we do music, how we dance (not my gift), how we speak, how we code-switch across contexts. "Code-switch" capacity presumes the cultural codes that "signify [a community's] most important shared agreements and values."[1] Framing the premises for the CRAFT method (Contact, Research, Action, Feedback, Teaching) of creating in community, Knight and Schwarzman continue: "For most of human history, these codes evolved *locally* through ethnic and family ties, schools, workplaces, friendships, religious and civic organizations. But over the last two centuries, since the advent of mass media, cultural codes have been controlled *remotely.*"[2] Thus, the community-based art process in part recovers "signs, symbols, rituals, and stories."[2] Theopoetic listening guides what I as a researcher do with the codes: how to perceive the value and stakes of the data. The academy exhorts scholars to make a contribution, so I listen for where the prophet Isaiah points me toward the Holy saying, "I am about to do a new thing; now it springs forth; do you not perceive it?" (Isa. 43:19 NRSV).

Expert qualitative researcher Johnny Saldaña frames the field as "approaches to and methods for the study of natural social life."[3] A prolific author and practitioner of theater, longitudinal qualitative inquiry, and ethnotheater,

---

1. Keith Knight and Mat Schwarzman, *Beginner's Guide to Community-Based Arts* (Oakland: New Village, 2005), xxix.

2. Knight and Schwarzman, *Beginner's Guide*, xxiii.

3. Johnny Saldaña, *Fundamentals of Qualitative Research: Understanding Qualitative Research* (New York: Oxford University Press, 2011), 3.

Saldaña describes possibilities of documenting, representing, and presenting study that include artistic outcomes as both process and product, thus generating significant epistemological mileage in research. My primary takeaway of how Saldaña offers methods for analyzing what researchers notice is that whether following models or creating models, the practices must be accessible, and the mechanisms must be available. Amid the landscape of accessible practice and available mechanisms, a qualitative researcher may code the data that they collect. The coding process organizes, groups, and categorizes data in order to manage, analyze, and eventually interpret and share the gathered information. Saldaña's *Coding Manual for Qualitative Researchers* is a leading resource for ethical and accessible coding practices that additionally offers insightful questions for considering coding strategies in relationship to the methodology of a study.[4] As a student of Saldaña's meticulous guidance, I acknowledge that my inquiry here may trespass the clear distinction he advocates between codes and themes.[5] I can only respectfully submit that I am responding to a unique and precious invitation from my editors and colleagues, so what I write here is a first cycle that I will continue to visit.

In my opening stories, the congregation and the classroom are natural settings. My sister and my classmate are both indigenous and observers; participant observers by immersion—or rather, my sister is participant observer as we visit houses of worship, while my classmate is one meaning-maker, and I am yet another as I add him into the dataset that I receive from the instructor. My tool is observation; his sounds are my criteria and measure. My classmate's "mm-hmm" parallels the self-reports from qualitative surveys or interviews and is a performance—an embodiment without rehearsal. Theopoetically, my research "question" arises from the listening. I did not know enough to go into the class with a research question. Yet the ever-present "How do I say this from the pulpit" is *always* the question: if my research question is any less important than a Sunday morning message, then I ought not be asking it.

METHODOLOGICAL APPROACHES THAT ATTUNE ME TO LISTENING THEOPOETICALLY

For me, listening theopoetically notices the everyday use of prayer language, scripture, hymnal phrases, congregational call and response behavior prac-

4. Johnny Saldaña, *The Coding Manual for Qualitative Researchers* (Los Angeles: Sage, 2009).
5. Saldaña, *Fundamentals of Qualitative Research*, 12.

ticed/applied in classes and rehearsals, and other codes of God-talk or God-thought or the valuing of personhood and human flourishing in my research contexts. *Doing* theopoetics invites me to value the stakes of those embedded everyday cues as epistemological in my coding and analysis. Prior to learning of theopoetics, I sought qualitative approaches that helped design research experiences that could collect such nuances.

The *Transformative* approach, a methodology helpful to listening theopoetically, advocates a perspectival shift on two fronts. First, it is looking for changes in society. Second, it may reference exploring change in each phase of the research design, data collection, and analysis. I welcome the notion of transformation as a descriptor of my work, should it be true. However, when first introduced to transformative language in qualitative analysis, I had no basis for empowering myself to remove established underpinnings of process and method. The language opened doors when I also wanted a call in some direction.

Collaborative Autoethnography (CAE) as developed by Heewon Chang, Faith Wambura Ngunjiri, and Kathy-Ann C. Hernandez is an approach that scaffolds multiple qualitative pathways. Where ethnography studies the shared practices, values, and beliefs of a culture, society, or social group, and autoethnographic methods consider the self in context, Chang, Ngunjiri, and Hernandez submit a holistic approach to social location and cultural embeddedness. "We define CAE as a qualitative research method in which researchers work in community to collect their autobiographical materials and to analyze and interpret their data collectively to gain a meaningful understanding of sociocultural phenomena as reflected in their autobiographical data."[6] I am especially partial to the visual mapping of culturegrams, kinsgrams, sociograms, and professional networks[7] that the collaborators utilize to represent relational spheres.

Constructivist research designs inquiry that builds theory from the investigation. In this practice, realities emerge from the process and participant experiences, instead of reality being something that already "is." Saldaña describes the related qualitative research genre of grounded theory, an iterative coding process that "works toward achieving a core or central category that conceptually represents what the study is all about."[8] I place the aims of constructivist and grounded theory approaches in dialogue with contemporary

6. Heewon Chang, Faith Wambura Ngunjiri, and Kathy-Ann C. Hernandez, *Collaborative Autoethnography* (Walnut Creek, CA: Left Coast Press, 2013), 24.

7. Chang, Ngunjiri, and Hernandez, *Collaborative Ethnography*, 81.

8. Saldaña, *Fundamentals of Qualitative Research*, 7.

youth studies scholars.[9] While the methods of these scholars vary, their ethical commitments to foregrounding childhood lived experiences inspire me to hold this strategy on my radar.

Convivial research deploys "investigative strategies that amplify local, situated, and poetic knowledges through *transdisciplinary* open-source technologies."[10] The richness and thickness of the convivial approach includes the markers of "co-generating knowledge that shares analysis about the actors, projects, networks, and strategies operating within a situated relation of force."[11] Open-source technologies resonate with the values of accessibility and availability that I receive from Saldaña, and I receive "force" as inviting me to engage the ongoing centrality of Divine Imagination in the spaces where I study and practice.

Arts-based approaches are practices of both collecting and reporting data. Patricia Leavy describes this method as applied "during all phases of social research" and names disrupting traditional paradigms as one goal of arts-based research.[12] For example, embodied work, such as image theater,[13] which thematically sculpts bodies in space to "bodystorm," is an arts-based strategy for analyzing a concept. One liberative aspect is that the practice frees participants from words, from "getting them right," and the exercise progresses democratically among participants. The work yields the language *after* the embodied analysis of a concept. Describing the free associations of sculpted bodies parallels captioning a photograph: added language yields from a progression of input.

How Listening Theopoetically Could Look and Sound

One of my favorite archives is a photo of a research site's trash cans overflowing with food packaging remnants. I took the photo before I had ever heard the word

9. Robin Bernstein, *Racial Innocence: Performing American Childhood from Slavery to Civil Rights* (New York: New York University Press, 2011); Stephani Etheridge Woodson, *Theatre for Youth Third Space: Performance, Democracy, and Community Cultural Development* (Bristol, UK: Intellect, 2015); Evelyn Parker, *The Sacred Selves of Adolescent Girls: Hard Stories of Race, Class, and Gender* (Cleveland: Pilgrim, 2006); Almeda Wright, *The Spiritual Lives of Young African Americans* (New York: Oxford University Press, 2017).

10. Manuel Callahan, *Convivial Research*, spring 2018 (San Jose: Center for Convivial Research & Autonomy), 1, http://cril.mitotedigital.org/sites/default/files/content/ccra_con vivial_research_2-18.pdf.

11. Callahan, *Convivial Research*, 1.

12. Patricia Leavy, *Method Meets Art: Arts-Based Research Practice* (New York: Guilford, 2009), 2–3.

13. Augosto Boal, *Theatre of the Oppressed* (New York: Theatre Communications, 1985).

"theopoetic," yet theopoetic listening describes my ability to recognize the depth of information embedded in the image. The trash told the story of breaking bread together and of "feed[ing] my sheep" (see John 21:15–17 NRSV), of time spent gathered together, of anxieties and eating your feelings and comfort food and accompaniment and needs met. The trash was treasure that offered more nuance and *stakes of craving and hunger* than my Likert scale surveys ever could.[14]

I am transparently bringing a pastoral care approach to research. The arts kids who ate all those snacks are showing up in part to receive *care*, however the nurture is named. Post-pouring out their voices, youth poets need a chaplain backstage. Storytelling is caregiving for the community and ceremonial in offering. If I am using narrative inquiry, what story works for the liberation of Black people that does not have holy care and comfort in it? The process of acquiring that data must extend care as well. In the way that I trusted my classmate's response to the knowledge production that was happening and being shared in the service of the generative community, likewise the loop and cycle of process, the mirror that Alves assures us has something of us inside it,[15] must also feed care as it reflects and refracts in theopoetic collection and analysis. What community would deserve me showing up as a researcher and being "not pastoral" on purpose?

Admittedly, I have only gathered data with and concerning

- arts groups;
- youth arts groups;
- faith-based groups;
- faith-based arts groups;
- parents, leaders, counselors of arts/youth/faith-based groups;
- the US General Social Survey and the Survey of Public Participation in the Arts;
- reading archives (of arts groups, youth arts groups, faith-based groups . . .); and
- reading theory, theatre, and theology and their presence in public discourse.

Spaces bearing the premise of a holistic and embodied approach that counts the whole self as mattering for any inquiry are the places that call me and charge my research. Even as I confess that I have only presumed to research in spaces of shared liturgy, I also cannot think of anywhere that deserves any less comprehensive valuing of the core energy that propels its participants. I would

14. Likert scale survey formats typically ask research participants to respond on a five-point spectrum of strongly agree, agree, neither agree nor disagree, disagree, or strongly disagree.

15. Rubem A. Alves, *The Poet, the Warrior, the Prophet* (London: SCM, 2002).

like to believe that if I studied the science behind climate change or diabetes, I would still believe that the Lord cared about whether anything I am doing is going to help you. My research approaches prompt me to ask, *What part of you am I supposed to ignore?* Yes, Institutional Review Boards protect privacies; yes, I agree not to quote something you ask me not to; yes, at some point I face the seeming mundanity of "how many hours a week do you spend at your arts site" and you give me a number, yet my practice of collecting encounters you as a whole being who spends more time there than the work sessions require, or who wishes you could be there more, or is forced there more often than you want to be, or who misses because you are overscheduled or you have to work or attend to loved ones or your own self. Or you forget. Even with a number, how and why you gave that number matters, and that number is in relationship with all of the other responses to the question. Commonly in Black faith spaces, a leader exhorts, "You don't know what I've been through" or "You're looking at a miracle." Researching with children and youth, with their guardians, with artists, I carry with me the constellation of factors that conspired for each participant to show up and enable the work.

Thus, when asked to account for my work (such as in a grant application), part of me wants to write, "I didn't actually do anything. God sent them here like that." The theopoetic lens dances with the research approaches and maps "God sent them here like that" as an asset-based measure in the research design. That works if I ask and answer, "What gets to count as an asset?" For example, once "prayer warrior" is an asset, the theopoetic lens helps break down the literary skill, the vocal power and rhythmic cadences, the intellectually astute embedding of scripture, the navigation of call-and-response with the chorus of "yes Lords" and "amens" (or "facts!" which is what one social media post reported as the affirmation of blessing the food at Thanksgiving) as manifest data emerging amid a circle of bodies. Moreover, I take the liberty of saying that no prayer warrior confers the title upon themselves. The community bestows the role, with both humans and the Holy together as witnesses. My assessment measures might somewhat objectively include how frequently a participant is called upon to lead, open, or close out a meeting in prayer. I could tally that frequency as well as the mm-hmms and amens. Yet the theopoetic lens forges the next layer, the efficacy of the moment; the question of accomplishing "We won't leave here like we came" through the performative utterance[16] of the prayer and its elicited agreements.

16. J. L. Austin, *How to Do Things with Words* (Cambridge: Harvard University Press, 1962); Judith Butler, *Gender Trouble: Feminism and the Subversion of Identity* (New York: Routledge, 2006).

Like the arts-based model, then, the theopoetic lens manifests at all phases of research design, data collection, analysis, and reporting, operating structurally and literarily. Augusto Boal, author of *Theatre of the Oppressed*, rejects poetics that only allow one person to be the protagonist. For Boal, a poetics of the oppressed allows a story to belong to a multitude; to a community; to a collective that wants each other's good, intertwined, as centrality. I too advocate for arts practices to count as literary language. Likewise, I also advocate for including how our bodies and senses recognize and share encounters with the Divine as literacies and cultural competencies in God-talk and Theo-thought. Tangibly, prayer is poetry that facilitates an epistemological process as it unfolds. I stand on how the writer of Luke-Acts describes the day of Pentecost: I allow that shared faith community and shared faith concepts activate understanding that is heard, felt, and seen.

Leaning into the day of Pentecost could invite boundary and bias questions between imposing my own sacred texts or theology(ies), crediting participants with their inputs, and listening theopoetically. For me, the practices that accuse such binaries are the very interstices which invoke the need for (a) the strategies that I outline at the start of this chapter and (b) theopoetic listening that is big enough to hold many transdisciplinary languages in one communal container and invite multifaceted, mixed-methods analysis, according to context and community. Even researching inside of congregational spaces and faith-based institutes cannot presume what anyone believes.

The capacious God-talk I am listening for is that of Creator, of imagination, of story theology and theological anthropology, intersecting qualitative methods, biblical exegesis, and dramaturgy. A chaplaincy practice of story theology is to hear a story—any story—and listen for where God is present in that story. Here I lean on Fujimura's concepts of culture care and theology of making.[17] Fujimura describes culture care as caring for the soul, stewarding community as one might tend to a garden. For Fujimura, this language allows cultural partners of differing beliefs to seek communal needs together and responds to our present cultural divisiveness. Theopoetics invites reckoning with the presence or absence of collaboratively pressing forward, problem-solving, and belonging and then points us toward creative response.

Theopoetic listening highlights my ongoing wrestling with the "double-consciousness"[18] of race and faith. My raced faith inextricably ties to my free-

---

17. Makoto Fujimura, *Culture Care: Reconnecting with Beauty for Our Common Life* (Downers Grove, IL: IVP Books, 2017); *Art and Faith: A Theology of Making* (New Haven: Yale University Press, 2020).

18. W. E. B. DuBois, *The Souls of Black Folk* (New York: Bantam Books, 1989).

dom to read and write at all, which would have been forbidden for me as recently as in my great-grandfather's lifetime. Navigating the externality of academic doublespeak regarding my insider-ness, otherness, bias, objectivity, and subjectivity elicits my attraction to and deep need for the liberative mirror methods that I explore in this chapter. Where I come from, bias would be erasing God from people's stories. My practice of the theopoetic lens honors a relationality that understands the self as created by the Holy and understands the self as cocreator. The relational underpinning inscribes responsibility, extends trust, insists on imagination as given circumstance. The "empirical evidence" I offer myself? "The people wouldn't have talked to me and played my theater games if I didn't come correct." I am here to honor the cocreative task that calls me to carve space that facilitates how folks share their gift, connect their gift to others, and tell the story of engaging that gift. My sacred work is tied to seeing neighbor as a created somebody.

Through my methodology, I am trying to "see the God in you"/"see you as God sees you" as a researcher. My meaningful cultural code liberates me to design my work—which then leans on Acts 2 and the methods outlined here for iterative collaborative process to translate "being seen" to contextual relevance, and the shared language outcome of that literary imagination will be the result of a theopoetic process. My father says that my Granny Trent taught him, "You can say anything you want to anyone you want. You just have to figure out *how* to say it." I wish I had followed my Aunt Ernestine around with a tape recorder; she could say anything to anybody with the *lovingkindness* that echoes when I see that word in scripture. Listening theopoetically is what the ancestors knew: if we didn't create a sacred circle, a safe/enough/brave space, then whatever *needed* to be said wasn't going to get said! Thus, doing theopoetics means sacralizing what we're going to do going in. It means if the unearthing of the data is digging up hard things, then my charge is to craft liturgy that cares for us when we set the shovels down. Making research practice "accessible" means inviting participation toward language and vocabulary that welcomes however people come to the table, identifying what undergirds, knowing what rituals root in the community, designing connectedness, intersecting the space.

Researching theopoetically exacts the care of designing liturgy: data collection with focus groups as sacred circles. With call-and-response, and time for reflection. Research during or as fellowship; as check-in at youth group. How might methods be liturgical uplift of sacred story and felt needs? How is the research a liturgy of care, a promise of having been seen and heard with assurance of action to come? How does the research mirror back to folks who chaplain themselves and each other by sharing, collating, interpreting, cocreating qualitative data in this way?

One early interview experience unexpectedly taught me the care needed to structure for participants to feel seen and heard: I was trying to interview a group of children who were already carefully conditioned to keep their concerns to themselves. Asking them questions yielded almost nothing. I then asked if they had questions for me . . . and suddenly I learned everything they cared about! An infectious energy moved through the group as they emboldened one another with their questions, eliciting one another's laughter, courage, and willingness to let their peers and teachers know what occupied their minds.

Research design means carving experience that allows me to read the mm/mm-hmm and the heave of a shoulder weighted or unburdened. I want to understand data collection as a laying at the foot of the cross, at an altar to call on Jesus together. In practice, that looks like embodiments of image theater, in sacred space or at sacred time as a community defines, with music, with time for call-and-response, silence and reflection, arts exercises that invite imagining and creating, real-time data feedback loop, collaborative exegesis, those devising and theater of the oppressed adapted practices. I often use the common Poster-Post-It–data-collection strategy of poster-size paper with relevant headings on a wall, granting participants the freedom, the option, the prompt to place Post-It notes with their comments related to the topics, and then supply them further with colored dots to "Vote for" or "Like" or "Amen" the comments of others. The experience is intentionally embodied, intentionally transparent, intentionally communal. It is intentionally invitational. Time, music, contextual space, silence, or improvisational response are all design opportunities for this practice.

WHEN I CODE

I notice cues of breath and behavior; who rolled their eyes and who sat on whose lap and who is making the snacks in the kitchen. I note that somebody brought kids of single-digit ages to the open mic and so either this is a family space in this church annex or the stakes are just that high that the kids are here in spite of *or because of* all that might go down and you still believe God's got them and you.

I code the audience sounds as congregational responses to the poetic healing work and lament traditions marked by phrases of hymns and civil rights songs. My theopoetic ear is recognizing that intertwined integration and how respondents learned such literary weaving from someone older and maybe very old. I code the embodiment of "feed my sheep" and that somebody knows that Word when the snacks come out. I document exhales, and rest, and putting on armor, and room for the Spirit . . . how people take turns and who dominates dialogue and who finds windows and spaces to insert their words, and I am designing liturgies for balance.

When a voice trails off . . . I want to value that, even if I cannot decipher "why" the voice fades. I can note impact. I can write an analytic memo[19] about the "chain of moments"—what triggered the trail, the moment before, like I do as a theater director, and then I can look at what happened after, and there's impact. It is not like "well they didn't finish their thought so there's nothing there." There is weight, or loss, or resonance, or restraint . . . there is *something*. The moment itself matters. And in community, the response to that trailing off call, is data. I record the sounds on the street outside and how you each got here and how you will get home safely.

What is it to transcribe recorded interviews or focus groups and insert punctuation? To make meaning visually with the output? How do I discern the capital letters of a word? While the non-theopoetic researcher has to make the same transcriptive choices that I do, what is the lens for where a sentence starts and stops? In theater courses and rehearsals, acting choices and script analysis, liturgies and the proclaiming of scripture, I remind my students that

> ellipses . . .
> and colons:
> and semicolons;
> and commas,
> and hyphens–
> *SOUND* different in the air
> The poet chooses
> visual sound / much like
> some sacred text
> is poetry
> and some is prose. How do we let the Holy guide us to represent
> the beauty and grace of a Participant
> choosing
> Choosing
> CHOOSING
> To help us / our-their community
> Contribute something [new]?
> *I didn't do anything. God sent them here like that.*

---

19. Saldaña, *Fundamentals of Qualitative Research*, 98.

Works Cited

Alves, Rubem A. *The Poet, the Warrior, the Prophet.* London: SCM, 2002.

Austin, J. L. *How to Do Things with Words.* Cambridge: Harvard University Press, 1962.

Bernstein, Robin. *Racial Innocence: Performing American Childhood from Slavery to Civil Rights.* New York: New York University Press, 2011.

Boal, Augusto. *Theatre of the Oppressed.* New York: Theatre Communications, 1985.

Butler, Judith. *Gender Trouble: Feminism and the Subversion of Identity.* New York: Routledge, 2006.

Callahan, Manuel. *Convivial Research.* Spring 2018. San Jose: Center for Convivial Research & Autonomy. http://cril.mitotedigital.org/sites/default/files/con tent/ccra_convivial_research_2-18.pdf.

Chang, Heewon, Faith Wambura Ngunjiri, and Kathy-Ann C. Hernandez. *Collaborative Autoethnography.* Walnut Creek, CA: Left Coast Press, 2013.

DuBois, W. E. B. *The Souls of Black Folk.* New York: Bantam Books, 1989.

Etheridge Woodson, Stephani. *Theatre for Youth Third Space: Performance, Democracy, and Community Cultural Development.* Bristol, UK: Intellect, 2015.

Fujimura, Makoto. *Art and Faith: A Theology of Making.* New Haven: Yale University Press, 2020.

———. *Culture Care: Reconnecting with Beauty for Our Common Life.* Downers Grove, IL: IVP Books, 2017.

Knight, Keith, and Mat Schwarzman. *Beginner's Guide to Community-Based Arts.* Oakland: New Village, 2005.

Leavy, Patricia. *Method Meets Art: Arts-Based Research Practice.* New York: Guilford, 2009.

Parker, Evelyn. *The Sacred Selves of Adolescent Girls: Hard Stories of Race, Class, and Gender.* Cleveland: Pilgrim, 2006.

Saldaña, Johnny. *The Coding Manual for Qualitative Researchers.* Los Angeles: Sage, 2009.

———. *Fundamentals of Qualitative Research: Understanding Qualitative Research.* New York: Oxford University Press, 2011.

Wright, Almeda. *The Spiritual Lives of Young African Americans.* New York: Oxford University Press, 2017.

5

A Theopoetic Method

Four Movements

TAMISHA A. TYLER

For a good portion of my life, I have identified as a foodie. I love food. I love trying out new cuisines, discovering new dishes, and if I could, most of my traveling would consist of food tours. But more than just food, I love cooking. There's something about being in the kitchen that calms me; it is a form of therapy. When I'm stressed, I just grab a recipe and ingredients, put on some music, and lose myself in a culinary experience. While I find that cooking usually comes naturally to me, baking is another story.

A little more of a science than an art, baking didn't come as naturally to me as cooking did. When I'm cooking, I find that leaning on my intuition helps me to create magic in the kitchen. This was not the case when I started baking. Baking has a way of showing your hand whether you like it or not. Didn't cream the eggs and sugar long enough? Cakes and cookies become flat and dense. Use butter at the wrong temperature, and a whole host of problems can occur. But when you get it right? Well, just think about your favorite baked good. You know what I'm talking about.

Now two things are probably happening: first, I've made you hungry, and second, you are wondering what this has to do with a theopoetic method. Well, unfortunately I can't do anything about the first problem so let's tackle the second. When we hear the words "method" and "methodology," we often think that they are interchangeable when they are in fact quite different. In the simplest of terms, *a method can be considered the ingredients of your re-*

search, while a methodology is the reason for research. Taking the metaphor of baking, one can say that a method consists of the ingredients and tools (not just the flour, butter, and sugar but also the pan, mixer, etc.). A methodology, however, concerns the reasoning behind these choices. It causes me to pause and ask questions like, "Why bake a cake? Why mix the eggs and butter before adding flour? Why use that pan, or that type of flour?" A methodology also provides a framework for how to go about answering these questions. For example, when I make my gluten-free banana cupcakes with Nutella cream cheese frosting, I am engaging several tools and ingredients, as well as histories and frameworks. The tools and ingredients I use like bananas and Nutella, as well as the muffin tin and foil paper, help me create the cupcakes themselves. But my methodology is what provides me with a framework that allows me to identify these baked goods as cupcakes in the first place. In this case, they are little personal cakes of equal size and shape that contain a specific set and amount of ingredients. There are other cakes that historically fit the description, but I learned about them as "cupcakes" and so that's how I articulate them. My methodology also names the background assumptions and commitments that guide all my baking efforts. For instance, I grew up in a home shaped by Southern culture, and I had a lot of siblings, so I learned to make large portions of things. And my Southern and Christian background shape the way I view hospitality, which is why my gluten-free choices show awareness of those who are generally left out of cupcake consumption because of gluten intolerance, thereby making my choice inclusive of those on the "culinary margins." My framework and lens are the histories and memories behind my questions (or methodology), while the tools and ingredients (or methods) help me address and shape the thing I am questioning. Thus, both "methodology" and "method" are important to consider as two different terms.

In this chapter I will share my four-part theopoetic method. I will begin this by first defining what I mean when I say "theopoetics." In the simplest of terms, *theopoetics is the creative, embodied practices and rhythms that help us articulate sensibilities about the divine.* My methodology is shaped by a lot of different disciplines, and so the method helps me to understand how those things work together tangentially. This theopoetic method is specifically a hermeneutical method, a method of interpretation. Even more, it is a *theopoetic* hermeneutical method, an interpretation that has a theopoetic lens and commitments. These are commitments beyond histories and beliefs that shape who I am; they represent the essence of our foundational question. To focus on a theopoetic hermeneutical method is to rest your foundation of inquiry in questions about the divine. While historians ask questions about the history of events of a particular phenomenon, or sociologists ask questions about the relation of peoples, a theologian's questions focus on the spiritual, transcendent, or ways that help us understand the divine. Even though this method pulls from various disciplines, its central focus will always be theological matters.

I often describe my method in four movements: social location, radical inquiry, theological inquiry, and artistic response. This method attempts to create a fluidity that captures the dynamics within each movement and their relationship to each other. Though the movements are numbered, they do not necessarily relate to a step-by-step process but are points of entry that should encourage practitioners to hold all four movements with the same weight. These movements are based in the spaces of both artistic creations and theology. They seek to name the realization that even the things I reject shape me, and just as I am shaped, other things are shaped. Octavia Butler says it best when she states, "All that you touch you change. All that you change changes you."[1] This work owes a great debt to her brilliance. The methodology represents why it is that these movements are necessary, but the methods themselves keep us in the constant dance of being a fully recognized person with histories stepping into a world of the trace, which is an imprint that an artifact leaves on culture that I will explain more fully later, and allowing that on the ground connection to be able to shape questions and observations.

In undertaking this method, I recognize that engaging in these movements is never done perfectly, but instead is a constant progress of growth and development, which is why I call them movements in the first place. Allow me to use a metaphor to explain. Recently, a friend asked if I could watch *Dancing with the Stars* with them as part of our quarantine ritual. Each week we were delighted by the various themes and costumes and cheered on our favorites as they attempted to master the cha-cha or tango. We learned together from the judges, who judged on classic ballroom technique and performance. In learning these new forms of dance, celebrities had to remember several things: the pace of step, the elevation of the elbows, the position of the head, and the connection with their partner, all while maintaining a smile. If they were dinged for not keeping their elbow up one week, they may receive praise for mastering it the next week. But in focusing on their elbow height, they would forget to be light on their feet or to place their head properly.

I imagine that maintaining each of the movements we will address is a similar process. Sometimes we get so focused on social location that we forget to include the artistic contributions of the trace. Or we are set on creating

---

1. Octavia E. Butler, *Parable of the Sower* (New York: Grand Central, 2019), 3.

alternative and creative forms of inquiry that we are left with shallow offerings of theological inquiry. It is only as we grow in this practice of methodology that our movements become intuitive; they become so embodied that the moment we step into that space of research, the work takes on its own life.

Movement One: Social Location

The first movement is social location. To understand social location is to recognize my own social location as well as the social location of the trace. The term "trace" is one I borrowed from Dr. Kutter Callaway. A trace includes not only the artifact, but also the imprint that an artifact leaves on culture. This can be a canceled TV show whose content is the subject of discussion years after it airs. It could also be a theme recurring throughout history that an artifact seeks to name. An example of this is the documentary film *13th*, which seeks to show how slavery shifts and morphs into aspects of criminality through mass incarceration. The film is the artifact, but it addresses the trace, which comes up at various points (slavery, the Thirteenth Amendment itself, incarceration of Black and Brown bodies, new technological ways of house arrest, etc.). Another example is hip-hop music. One song (an artifact) can spark a conversation about Black expression, oppression, police brutality, and censorship, thus touching upon several traces at once. The artifacts we examine do not exist only in the form that we are examining; in fact nothing exists that way. They are constantly moving and engaging with the world, changing because of technology and changes in culture, as well as through our engagement with them. Because of this, I will use the term "artifact" to speak to the piece of art or phenomena as it is, and I will use the term "trace" when speaking to the world that the artifact creates.

As such, an artifact comes from a world and creates a world. Similarly, so does the researcher. As a human, the researcher has a history and background that they bring to their interaction and interpretation of the trace. Moreover, a researcher brings questions and motivations that drive those questions. The questions a researcher asks are shaped by who they are. Even as we imagine new worlds, our imaginations are tethered to the very things we may want to change or try to escape. An example of this tethering comes from my very good friend Christopher Slatoff. Chris is a sculptor and lives in the Los Angeles area. He specializes in creating religious art and life-sized sculptures, which can be seen in various places across Southern California. We first met in a master's course on the Gospels, my first class in seminary. Chris was giving a presentation on the Gospels and art and offered a great example on how we view interpretation. He says: "I'm not sure if any of you are old enough to remember this but I remember when I saw some of the great movies about the life of Jesus or the Ten Commandments. I remember watching them thinking 'Oh yes, this is exactly what it looked like during biblical times!' I would then come back to the movie years later and say to myself 'Oh that was so 80s!' Or 'I can totally tell what decade that was made!'"[2]

What Chris is alluding to is the fact that even as we imagine past or future circumstances, the way we envision them is still tied to the things we currently see. In other words, our imaginations are tethered to our contexts. This does not mean that we can't move beyond them or that we can't create spaces and worlds that invoke change. It simply means that we do not do that work in a vacuum. We cannot untangle ourselves from our realities, and it is because of this that the best thing we can do is to acknowledge them. Naming our social location then becomes an exercise of the inevitable, a recognition of the water we swim in so that we can honor our limitations and foundations of inquiry.

This step of social location is more than the world of the trace or the world of the researcher but begins the process of what happens when those worlds collide. This is important in that it helps to create moments of resonance and dissonance between the researcher and the trace. In thinking of resonance, the researcher has the space to name what drew them to this trace, or how this trace helps them to address their overall questions of inquiry or honor their methodology. There also may be cultural resonance in various forms, and naming these connections can give great insight into a research project. What's more, it also helps to name potential blind spots a researcher may have with the trace they are investigating. For example, if I am engaging in my recipe of macaroni and cheese, I would have deep resonance in that it represents deep cultural and familial ties, and offering this close perspective can give great insight. At the same time, because it is something that is so close, I can miss the ways that others view and can speak into how that artifact lives in the world. This is not to say that one opinion is greater than the other but to name the fact that both resonance and dissonance are required in offering well-rounded research, even if the focus is in naming the realities of one or the other (resonance or dissonance).

2. Christopher Slatoff, lecture given in New Testament: Gospels course, taught by Tommy Givens, Fuller Theological Seminary, spring 2011.

Just as there are blind spots from being too close to something, there are also assumed responsibilities when engaging with something outside of your cultural expression.

Movement Two: Radical Inquiry

The second movement is that of radical inquiry. Like the first movement, radical inquiry takes the time to dig deeper into the realities of social location, especially as it relates to the world of interpretation. Radical inquiry engages interlocutors, offers critique of other forms of investigation of the trace, and helps the researcher engage with the trace in new ways. There are four steps to radical inquiry. These steps come from the work of Cathy Nutbrown and Peter Clough, who spent years teaching methodology, and their text *A Student's Guide to Methodology*. In their text discussing radical inquiry, they engage in four steps: radical looking, radical listening, radical reading, and radical questioning.

Nutbrown and Clough argue that research is persuasive, purposive, positional, and political.[3] Each of these movements engage in all four of these ideas, though they are most apparent in movement two. Through the process of radical inquiry, we can name and clarify our agenda, our position, and the impact our research will have on the greater public.

Our first look into radical inquiry is radical looking or making the familiar strange. We learned in movement one that there are resonances between the researcher and the trace, and radical looking acknowledges the challenge of this by offering tools of reimagining how to engage. Radical looking does not negate the resonances; however, it simply serves as an invitation of exploration beyond that which is familiar (this is also a good point for each of the steps in radical inquiry). Using the analogy of a traveler who encounters familiar things in new ways and cultures, Clough and Nutbrown define radical looking this way: "All researchers need to develop the capacity to see their topic with *new and different lenses* in order to look beyond and transform their own current knowledge. Topics present themselves for research in different ways and for all sorts of different reasons. What distinguishes research from everyday interest or curiosity, however, is the *opening up of familiar things to alternative ways of seeing*."[4]

---

3. Peter Clough and Cathy Nutbrown, *A Student's Guide to Methodology: Justifying Enquiry*, 3rd ed. (Los Angeles: Sage, 2012), 11.
4. Clough and Nutbrown, *A Student's Guide to Methodology*, 72, emphasis added.

This makes the practice of observation key. Though a widely used research method, the practice of observation is curated and contained by the four realities of research (purpose, persuasiveness, positionality, and politics). That is, two people can see the same thing, but have very different observations based on what they seek to ultimately accomplish, how they will convince others of their project's importance, their own social location, and the implications for change in the greater society. All this shapes the way we see, and the practice of observation names that specificity. Therefore, radical looking isn't just looking at something (evidence), it is also a *looking for* (meaning), a looking with the acknowledgment and intent of the agendas, histories, and imaginations that shape both the trace and researcher.

Next is the act of radical listening. Radical listening deals with issues of voice. This is primarily the voice of the researcher as we continue to articulate the ways that research is positioned and political. This centering of voice not only reinforces movement one but deals with the implications of the relationship between the researcher and research. Radical listening addresses the role of distance (and dissonance) in research, asks questions that relate to our positioning (how close are you to your question?), and considers ways to include our own voice while weighing the risk of being "too close."[5] To listen is to pay attention to the implications of our voice, but it also considers the actions that result from our listening as well as the voices of those we are investigating and others who have spoken into the world of the trace.

In thinking about the other voices in a research project, interpretation is key. When a researcher acknowledges certain voices above others, chooses interlocutors, or focuses on certain arguments, they are ultimately engaging in modes of interpretation and curation. Part of the responsibility of the researcher is to offer a clear and ethical perspective, both in their own voice and in the voices with which they choose to engage. Radical listening challenges the researcher not only to engage voices that are comfortable or familiar but also to seek out voices that are different, especially voices that have been historically marginalized.

The third aspect of radical inquiry is radical reading. "Radical reading provides the justification for the critical adoption or rejection of existing knowl-

---

5. I recognize that ideas of being "too close" can often relate to a perceived objectivity that completely negates the understanding of social location in movement one. This is not in support of an underlying assumption of an objectivity that is supported by the assumption of White normativity, but an understanding of what happens when the world of the researcher and the world of the trace collide.

edge and practices."[6] You will notice that each aspect of radical inquiry builds off the last. If radical listening is the acknowledgment of voice (both researcher and others), radical reading reinforces the justification behind the voices that are given authority in a certain project.

One of the primary ways that this is done is through criticality, or "being critical." Criticality serves as a pillar of research for several reasons. First, it helps to establish the justification behind the relationship between other scholars and their work. Second, it establishes a history and acknowledgment of scholarship that a researcher enters at the beginning of their project. Radical reading helps to create the perimeters and frameworks around the researcher and their trace by acknowledging and engaging the world of research that informs both. As an ethical act, the researcher must honor prior work, whether by accepting or rejecting its findings before they can offer their own contributions.

One thing that is important in radical reading as a theopoetic method is to honor the fact that aspects of research are not found only in books. This will become most evident in our final movement, but it is worth noting here that reading isn't the only form of information consumption; thus, information through aspects of reading only limits the possibilities of research. Engagment with various modalities (including, but not limited to, visual art, storytelling, dance, and histories of oral tradition) is critical and necessary for a theopoetic method.

The final aspect of radical inquiry is radial questioning. Clough and Nutbrown describe it by saying, "Radical questioning reveals not only gaps in knowledge, but why and how answers might be morally and politically necessitated."[7] Radical questioning concludes the aspect of radical inquiry by addressing the findings surrounding radical looking, listening, and reading and articulating gaps in knowledge by asking questions about the critical and ethical implications of the inquiry. This aspect also helps to narrow down and clarify research questions that come out of these findings.

MOVEMENT THREE: THEOLOGICAL INQUIRY (ASKING THE GOD QUESTION)

The third movement is that of asking the god question or theological inquiry. As stated above, since this is a theopoetic hermeneutical method, theological

---

6. Clough and Nutbrown, *A Student's Guide to Methodology*, 106.
7. Clough and Nutbrown, *A Student's Guide to Methodology*, 140.

inquiry serves as the central contribution. There are two central questions to this movement. The first is, What does god say about this? This basic question represents the normative or traditional approach to theological inquiry. In a traditional sense, a theologian brings theological resources to bear on an artifact. Using a particular religious history or tradition, scripture, reason, or personal experience, a researcher then engages how these theological tools offer insight into a trace. This aspect of this movement represents a certain hermeneutical flow, situating of research (researcher and trace), critiquing fields of knowledge (radical inquiry), offering contribution (theological engagement), and engaging with findings and implications (artistic responses).

What makes this movement unique, however, is that the second aspect of theological inquiry *reverses* the hermeneutical flow by offering voice to the artifact itself. The question, What does god say about this? then becomes, What does *this* say about god? This second question allows the artifact to speak into the realities of the theological sources of the researcher specifically, and of theology more generally. Since theology itself is a semiotic system, giving the trace voice and authority to offer insight into theological realities acknowledges the fact that culture already informs our theological inquiry, and seeks to name those possibilities in clear and concrete ways.

This aspect of theological inquiry is not only about the ways humanity interacts with the divine. Because our thoughts on the divine can often serve as foundational for our ideas about everything else, theological inquiry also names how our theologies shape our understanding of the human condition and interaction with each other, as well as ecological realities and ways to engage with the environment and other species.

Movement Four: Artistic Response

The fourth and final movement deals with responding artistically. This movement draws directly from a theopoetic context and seeks to continue in the vein of honoring the relationship between researcher and trace. It also serves to continue the role of radical inquiry, particularly that of radical listening, or voice. Traditionally, research findings result in articles or books that seek to offer clear insight into what was discovered because of the research. However, in addition to the reversal of theological hermeneutical flow, I suggest that a true theopoetic method is not complete unless it leaves room for findings to be offered in the same modalities as the object of research itself. Responding artistically becomes a method of engagement in two ways. First, it is a method that seeks to use the arts to articulate findings of research. To elaborate on this point, social research scholar Patricia Leavy offers insight into arts-based research (ABR), including narrative inquiry and dance/movement as a methodological innovation. According to Leavy, ABR can be defined as "a transdisciplinary approach to knowledge building that combines the tenets of the creative arts in research contexts."[8] Her work as a scholar and as an artist serves as an inroad into the possibilities of ABR with a theological lens. It is my suggestion that a theopoetic method seeks to bring these two fields into conversation.[9]

Second, this movement looks to center works of art (that is, other artifacts) that are inspired by or engage the artifact that is being researched. If we are to understand the artifact as a trace (or the world that the artifact both creates and inhabits), then looking to other forms of art that shape the context of our scope of research is critical. It is also important to the trace to bear witness to how the artifact has inspired more art. As an example of such inspiration, *Octavia's Brood* is a collection of short stories written by community activists and organizers as a way to honor Octavia Butler. If Butler's work or Butler herself becomes the point of research, then this collection of short stories serves as part of the trace, or the world created by Butler. In other words, paying attention to the way that art is both inspired by and begets other art serves as an important lens in a theopoetic method.

CONCLUSION

This chapter presented a theopoetic method in four movements: social location, radical inquiry, theological inquiry, and artistic response. Each of these movements seeks to help us establish the creative and embodied rhythms and practices that help us articulate sensibilities about the divine. While I do not believe that this method is exhaustive, I do believe it is a rich starting point for how theopoetic methodological inquiry can offer much to the overall field of theology and religion.

8. Patricia Leavy, ed., *Handbook of Arts-Based Research* (New York: Guilford, 2019), 4.

9. I write more on this in my dissertation, "Articulating Sensibilities: Methodologies in Theopoetics in Conversation with Octavia E. Butler" (PhD diss., Fuller Theological Seminary, July 2022), as I establish five methodological pillars of the field, one of which includes the creative. Though I don't get into Leavy's work extensively in the dissertation, Leavy becomes a major interlocular in many of my future projects, including a book version of the dissertation.

Works Cited

Butler, Octavia E. *Parable of the Sower*. New York: Grand Central, 2019.

Clough, Peter, and Cathy Nutbrown. *A Student's Guide to Methodology: Justifying Enquiry*. 3rd ed. Los Angeles: Sage, 2012.

Leavy, Patricia, ed. *Handbook of Arts-Based Research*. New York: Guilford, 2019.

Tyler, Tamisha A. "Articulating Sensibilities: Methodologies in Theopoetics in Conversation with Octavia E. Butler." PhD diss., Fuller Theological Seminary, 2022.

6

Theoespíritu as Pedagogy

Un Jale Bruto

CAROLINA HINOJOSA-CISNEROS

We live in a transformative time as we shift realities and jolt into new ones. We are all constructing new realities from COVID-19, a global pandemic that changed the lives of humanity and more-than-human kin globally as well as Texans on March 23, 2020, when the entire state went into lockdown after its first outbreak. In an emergency temporary order issued by Governor Greg Abbott, all in-person instruction halted. In a Texas Public Radio *Texas Matters* segment, journalist David Martin Davies explains, "Also, in that order, all Texas schools must close. In-person classrooms are no longer a thing, at least for now."[1] On March 23, 2020, the novel coronavirus created a *desmadre*—a chaotic state of being—revealing the digital divide within our marginalized communities.

Many educators made makeshift classrooms from their living rooms, kitchens, and washrooms. Access to the internet was critical to the continuity of education; not to mention the many families whose parents were considered essential workers and still had to show up to work with their children at home, left to figure out technology and virtual classroom learning on their own. My family, too, was impacted by this abrupt virtual shift in space. As Texans we

1. David Martin Davies, "Texas Matters: The Great Coronavirus Shutdown of 2020," *Texas Matters*, Texas Public Radio, March 23, 2020.

Un jale bruto translates to "hard work" from Spanish to English.

would endure a snow storm a few months later while learning to live in the new reality of a global pandemic. While we may never get back to the way life was pre-coronavirus, we know that our students and their families will yearn for an education that engages a holistic approach. How we shift language, create new methodologies, and make space for the sacred will leave an intergenerational scar. As an English instructor I can and should leave the soul prints of intentionality and wisdom by engaging in soul work, a holistic teaching that privileges the spirit in times where activism is necessary to move us out of a chaotic liminality. The classroom, virtual or physical, becomes cataclysmic, where imagination, hope, and struggle become commonplace. What, then, do students create from within the tension between hope and trauma? What negotiation takes place in order to create meaning as a form of survival both inside and outside of the classroom? Often, this creation is in the form of art, but it can also be rhetorical, spiritual, and epistemological. This chapter hopes to ground *theoespíritu*, a term derived from theopoetics I use as a holistic critical pedagogy toward reclaiming the tension between hope and trauma in the writing classroom. I am interested in imagining and articulating a new pedagogical framework that expands and builds upon theopoetics.

Theopoetics is an interdisciplinary field that combines elements of poetic analysis, narrative and process theologies, and postmodern philosophy. In its literal definition, theopoetics draws us closer to divine and ancestral knowledge making. Expanding this further, the divine is intertwined in the everydayness of many cultures, but especially minoritized communities where the spirit is not separate from personhood and the self. In his seminal text, *Way to Water: A Theopoetics Primer*, Callid Keefe-Perry indicates, "Theopoetics is a way of perceiving and expressing so as to more directly articulate how the Divine manifests in human experience of the world."[2] One of many human experiences can be encountered in classrooms. How we as educators approach that human experience hinges on the holistic theoretical framework we engage or do not engage in our classroom spaces. I argue that theopoetics is foundational to engaging in a critical pedagogy that moves the act of writing toward peaceful resistance. Through a theopoetic framework, educators become shamanistic healers who bring the student back to themselves as the pivotal starting point from which to create, synthesize, and relate to literature and writing in the spirit of Laura I. Rendón's *sentipensante* pedagogy and Gloria Anzaldúa's spiritual activism. Rendón's feeling-thinking pedagogy privileges spiritual intelligence as a holistic pedagogical practice. She posits,

2. Callid Keefe-Perry, *Way to Water: A Theopoetics Primer* (Cascade Books, 2014).

"I call Sentipensante (sensing/thinking) Pedagogy [that] which represents a teaching and learning approach based on wholeness, harmony, social justice, and liberation."[3] Her pedagogical approach is rooted in ancestral wisdom, harmony, and wholeness. Anzaldúa defines spiritual activism as "spirituality for social change, spirituality that recognizes the many differences among us, yet insists on our commonalities and uses these commonalities as catalysts for transformation."[4]

Theopoetics is a liberative praxis. When brought into the classroom theopoetics is a groundbreaking attempt to assist students in locating their cultural and linguistic wealth, in compounding their embodied, spiritual, and collective capital. One comes closest to divine wisdom (i.e., ancestral knowledge, or God) when one creates something (i.e., ex nihilo—something from nothing) that speaks to their everyday life and epistemological source(s). As a Chicana from the southside of Yanaguana, San Antonio, Texas, I look to liberation theologian Ada María Isasi-Díaz, who uses the term *lo cotidiano* as a key element in *mujerista* theology,[5] a liberatory theology for Hispanic women who felt unseen in patriarchal spaces like the priesthood. Mujerista theology gave Latina and Chicana women ample space to utilize their voices for holistic and systemic change in patriarchal spaces by drawing upon their everyday lives—lo cotidiano. In that vein, I use "theoespíritu" to wrestle with liminal space and everydayness, and to expand on language that was rendered inaccessible when formed out of, in, and within academic, theological, and patriarchal language.

Theoespíritu, a term I continue to shape, relocates rigid terminology within culture, privileges the spirit, and creates a portal of intergenerational healing between someone without access to academic language and the academy from where that language exists. Theoespíritu locates the Creator and the co-creation within the language of Chicana/o/x and Tejana/o/x literature and the everyday. Theoespíritu and spirituality are indivisible aspects of the borderland imaginary. Theoespíritu begins peace-ing our desmadre, or piecing together our chaos, as subjugated peoples in academic spaces who must survive as mothers, students, educators, and comrades. Our everydayness, lo cotidiano, becomes where we create personal narratives, literature, and iconography.

3. Laura I. Rendón, *Sentipensante (Sensing/Thinking) Pedagogy: Education for Wholeness, Social Justice, and Liberation* (Sterling, VA: Stylus, 2009), 132.

4. Gloria E. Anzaldúa, *Light in the Dark/Luz En Lo Oscuro: Rewriting Identity, Spirituality, Reality* (Durham, NC: Duke University Press, 2015).

5. Ada María Isasi-Díaz, *Mujerista Theology: A Theology for the Twenty-First Century* (Maryknoll, NY: Orbis, 1996).

Theoespíritu reimagines and amalgamates a spatial narrative into the "beyond" of Homi Bhabha, the "spiritual activism" of Gloria Anzaldúa, the "temporal geographies" of Mary Pat Brady, the "decolonial spaces" of Linda Tuhiwai Smith, the "differential consciousness" of Chela Sandoval, and the "sentipensante pedagogy" of Laura I. Rendón.[6] To articulate a peace-ing together of a reimagined space toward a liberative praxis, theoespíritu asks us to reimagine academic spaces as a spiritually grounded site of knowledge making. This chapter is a continuous work in progress and contains terminology I wish to continue theorizing as I begin writing my dissertation, contributing to book chapters, learning from my elders, and cocreating with other scholars.

The Necessity of Espíritu

In this present space, our ancestors are remembering us—an active act of narration. Indigenous writer Sherri Mitchell states, "When we connect with our ancestors and put their wisdom to action, we are evolving our collective consciousness. We are transporting the ancient truths of our collective past and birthing them into our future. What we create out of those truths extends the wisdom of all who have gone before us, and it provides a guide for all those who will follow."[7] A cocreative narrative of our present space is a collective effort. A response to this desmadre is the articulation of liminality that Ashley Theuring describes when she gives language to suffering in the face of tragedy. At the same time, the language of theology fails us. Theuring states, "Theopoetics can respond to suffering and give us language in the face of tragedy. . . . Theopoetics creates a potential space in which both hope and doubt can remain together, held in tension. This balance is important in the wake of trauma and suffering."[8] While Theuring uses theopoetics to respond to the Sandy Hook Elementary shooting, clearly stating that we can move too quickly into hope "absent of doubt [because] it may not be appropriate or helpful for

---

6. Mary Pat Brady, *Extinct Land, Temporal Geographics: Chicana Literature and the Urgency of Space* (Durham, NC: Duke University Press, 2002); Chela Sandoval, *Methodology of the Oppressed* (Minneapolis: University of Minnesota Press, 2000); Linda Tuhiwai Smith, *Decolonizing Methodologies: Research and Indigenous Peoples*, 2nd ed. (London: Zed, 2012).

7. Sherri Mitchell, *Sacred Instructions: Indigenous Wisdom for Living Spirit-Based Change* (Berkeley: North Atlantic Books, 2018), 13.

8. Ashley Theuring, "Holding Hope and Doubt: An Interreligious Theopoetic Response to Public Tragedies," *Cross Currents* 4, no. 64 (2014): 549–64.

those suffering deeply,"[9] she articulates a space outside of religious language to hold the tension between hope and trauma. In "Theopoetics: Process and Perspective," L. B. C. Keefe-Perry posits, "The term *theopoetics* was first seen in the form of *theopoeiesis*, used by Stanley Romaine Hopper in a 1971 speech that grew out of conversations that had been taking place within the Society for Art and Religion in Contemporary Culture and the American Academy of Religion. Since then, theopoetics has served as a noun referring to a particular devotional quality of a text, a genre of religious writing, and a postmodern perspective on theology. A useful working definition of the term would be the study of making God known through text."[10]

I have taken theopoetics from noun to verb, from the academy to every-dayness. From an English noun to a bilingual working term. Theoespíritu makes the divine known through personhood. When mujeristas and third space practitioners of theoespíritu cocreate theory, we also (re)locate termi-nology. Theoespíritu breaks apart, *despedasada*, like Coyolxauhqui, the Aztec goddess dismembered by her brother, the Aztec warrior god Huitzilopochtli, in order to cocreate within the liminality of her pieces. *Theo* is theory and the-ology intertwined like mirror images of one another. *Theo* is head and heart. *Espíritu* is the spirit in Spanish to draw us away from the Western gaze and inward toward our ancestors and the Holy Spirit—ancestral wisdom. *Tú* is the "you" that grounds us in the everyday. Theory, theology, ancestral wisdom, and the "you" create a narrative that seeks to relocate collective wisdom within an academic framework, language, and spiritual wisdom. When brought into the classroom, theoespíritu facilitates peacemaking and peace-ing together.

Why is espíritu necessary? Because it engages the "you" and the "spirit." Gloria Anzaldúa reminds us, "Spirituality is a different kind and way of know-ing. . . . Coming to terms with spirit means bringing yourself into harmony with the world within and around you. One finds one's way to spirit through woundings [like COVID-19],[11] through nature [the urge to grow new life, more *plantitas* to consume], through reading [sacred texts, poetry, *maestras*], through actions [staying at home to slow the spread or wearing facemasks in public during this pandemic], through discovering new approaches to prob-lems."[12] When we return to a (re)newed normality, as educators, parents, and

9. Theuring, "Holding Hope and Doubt," 552.

10. L. B. C. Keefe-Perry, "Theopoetics: Process and Perspective," *Christianity and Liter-ature* 58, no. 4 (Summer 2009): 579–600.

11. Parenthetical emphases are mine.

12. Anzaldúa, *Light in the Dark*, 38.

third-space practitioners, our students will need to speak of this wounding. Students will want to purge themselves of this *sufrimiento* (suffering). In Nahuatl, the term meant to give language to this suffering is *tlatoliniaya*—there was suffering. Though the suffering will seem to have passed, it will be something that lives with us. We must expunge these *aires*—ailments—from our bodies because we will continue to be in a state of *tlaihiyohuiliztli*—suffering. Those who will live to tell of this suffering will be in a *nepantla* state, a liminality, an in-between state. We will see double: pre- and post-COVID-19.

CIRCULAR HEALING IN THE CLASSROOM

In "Now Let Us Shift . . . Conocimiento . . . Inner Work, Public Acts," Anzaldúa posits, "Living between cultures results in 'seeing' double, first from the perspective of one culture, then from the perspective of another."[13] Relocating the spirit from its dislocation will allow us to cocreate a new narrative. Before a course in spatial theory, I would have said that this narrative would induce our healing; however, healing is a continuous process, and it is not linear. Indeed, healing is circular. Our geopolitical location further informs this. In *My Grandmother's Hands: Racialized Trauma and the Pathway to Mending Our Hearts and Bodies*, Resmaa Menakem states, "We heal primarily in and through the body, not just through the rational brain."[14] He further extrapolates nonbinary healing, which does not have to pit academic intelligence over spiritual intelligence. Healing can hold them both. As Menakem further unpacks and defines trauma and the trauma endured by African American and Black communities, he posits, "Resilience *can* be built and strengthened, both individually and collectively."[15] Theoespíritu, as a liberative pedagogy, can bridge and build individual and collective resilience in communities of color where trauma informs the lives of students entering classroom spaces, whether virtually or physically. It is a pedagogy with which we can currently engage. Theoespíritu is employed at different aspects and times because healing is circular.

How do we create peace in the classroom when war converges as the architecture, the monumental consciousness surrounding us, and from where

---

13. Anzaldúa, *Light in the Dark*, 117–59.

14. Resmaa Menakem, *My Grandmother's Hands: Racialized Trauma and the Pathway to Mending Our Hearts and Bodies* (Las Vegas: Central Recovery, 2017), 13.

15. Menakem, *My Grandmother's Hands*, 51.

first-generation students create scholarship? We are literally killing each other. Children are caged and families are separated at our southern border. Children are oppressed not only in the United States but also in Palestine, Iran, Central America, Mexico, and many other places worldwide. Our recent entanglement, an age-old entanglement with Iran, has proven that we are ready, at all costs, to place profit over people on the front lines (and headlines) of senseless wars. We are literally killing each other.

What does this have to do with the writing classroom? Professors of English, and most instructors, take on the task of peace-ing the desmadre by usurping our collective imagination toward a radical hybridization of consciousness where our students can write themselves into communal healing. Peace-ing a disaster, a war zone, like piecing Coyolxauhqui, an Aztec goddess dismembered by her brother, the Aztec god Huitzilopochtli, takes a spiritual undergirding to re-peace our dis(re)membered students and writing spaces. Our students need a different way of imagining the world and our place(s) within that world.

When educators, alongside students, enter into a hybridization of consciousness where the spiritual is foundational, where the collective imagination, the common unity (*commun-unidad*) of our institutions is common practice, a radical act of healing begins to take place; writing becomes a tool toward theoespíritu. bell hooks asserts what Paulo Freire affirms in education for liberation, "Education can only be liberatory when everyone claims knowledge as a field in which we all labor."[16] Our collective labor facilitates a collective conscious healing. Healing becomes communal.

Writing is not separated from the body, and the body is not separated from the spirit. When students look inward, they become agents of their own change. They search for a language to apply to their life experiences, which allows them to *peace* themselves together. First-generation students crave peace and healing from generational trauma, from the consequences of burning fires in California to the Amazon to Australia. Students crave healing from the experience or imagining of rupture when denied entry at our southern border, and again at the language border, and again at the academic border, and again in the job market border—each time surviving a *golpe*, a hit, that affects the body, spirit, and mind in various ways.

How is theopoetics relevant to the classroom and to the student who does not believe in a theology of divinity? Every classroom is not located in a seminary; what if we are in a public university or local library? In Rendón's

---

16. bell hooks, *Teaching to Transgress: Education as the Practice of Freedom* (New York: Routledge, 1994), 14.

Sentipensante (Sensing/Thinking) Pedagogy, Norma Elia Cantú reminds us, however, that "Whenever we work with writing, we're really working with spiritual things."[17] Theuring describes the language of theology that must make room for our lived epistemologies. She posits that "our religious language must speak from our experiences, or it will become meaningless."[18] Theology is joined to the everyday. The writing in our classrooms must speak from our students' experiences or it, too, will become meaningless. Students create a social theory to respond to historical events and social tragedies when they engage in meaning-making through writing. As educators, we must reimagine writing discourse. The spiritual intellect must be privileged in community to cultivate a sense of knowing.

CONCLUSION

I was a substitute instructor for an Applications of Learning Freshman Seminar. Having no prior knowledge of the students or the mechanics of the relationship between the classroom space and the student's inhabiting the space, I substituted for one class period. The class was to talk about their interpretation of a chapter from *All the Agents and Saints* by El Paso writer Stephanie Elizondo Griest. I guided the students to think critically by asking a few questions. I asked an initial question: "Since the author chose to speak about a miracle tree, do you have a metaphorical miracle tree in your life that helps you navigate college?" Most students answered as I drew a miracle tree on the whiteboard and wrote in their answers. One student could not answer. I probed, "Is your miracle tree your art?" She shook her head. "Is your miracle tree your journal?" She did not answer me, so I moved on, removing an uncomfortable spotlight from her. When everyone finished answering the miracle tree question, she spoke up, "I'm Native, so I think every tree is a miracle." The room went silent. The tension lifted. If every tree is a miracle, then every person is a miracle. Religion has nothing to do with that. "Ancestral ways of knowing [are] based on wholeness. . . . Faith and reason, as well as science and the divine, [are] not separate but viewed as two parts of a whole."[19]

Theoespíritu does not ask us to be complicit in the world's deficits. It asks us as students and educators what writing asks of us: to enter into a "trans-

17. Rendón, *Sentipensante (Sensing/Thinking) Pedagogy*, 80.
18. Theuring, "Holding Hope and Doubt," 550.
19. Rendón, *Sentipensante (Sensing/Thinking) Pedagogy*, 134.

formation of consciousness."[20] When COVID-19 relegated us to our homes, educators made do while grappling with the digital divide that affected us all, particularly our marginalized communities. Within the liminality of a pre- and post-COVID reality, we are creating new kinds of literatures, languages, and funds of knowledge and wrestling with what this means in the context of the Borderlands. Theoespíritu is a critical pedagogy grounded in working with things of the spirit like writing, creating, and locating ourselves within academic frameworks. Post-COVID, we must grapple with the desmadre left in the wake of a global pandemic on our marginalized communities. How will educators respond to the need of our students to overcome the violence created within this liminality? Theoespíritu, as critical pedagogy, calls us inward to theorize new realities to overcome this desmadre and to articulate our peace-ing.

Works Cited

Anzaldúa, Gloria E. *Light in the Dark/Luz En Lo Oscuro: Rewriting Identity, Spirituality, Reality*. Durham, NC: Duke University Press, 2015.

Brady, Mary Pat. *Extinct Land, Temporal Geographies: Chicana Literature and the Urgency of Space*. Durham, NC. Duke University Press, 2002.

Davies, David Martin. "Texas Matters: The Great Coronavirus Shutdown of 2020." *Texas Matters*. Texas Public Radio. March 23, 2020.

hooks, bell. *Teaching to Transgress: Education as the Practice of Freedom*. New York: Routledge, 1994.

Isasi-Díaz, Ada María. *En La Lucha/In the Struggle: Elaborating a Mujerista Theology*. Minneapolis: Fortress, 2004.

————. *Mujerista Theology: A Theology for the Twenty-First Century*. Maryknoll, NY: Orbis, 1996.

Keating, Ana Louise, and Gloria E. Anzaldúa, eds. *This Bridge We Call Home: Radical Visions for Transformation*. New York: Routledge, 2002.

Keefe-Perry, Callid. "Theopoetics: Process and Perspective." *Christianity and Literature* 58, no. 4 (2009): 579–600.

————. *Way to Water: A Theopoetics Primer*. Eugene, OR: Cascade Books, 2014.

Menakem, Resmaa. *My Grandmother's Hands: Racialized Trauma and the Pathway to Mending Our Hearts and Bodies*. Las Vegas: Central Recovery, 2017.

---

20. Mary Rose O'Reilley, *The Peaceable Classroom* (Portsmouth, NH: Boynton/Cook, 1993), 26.

Mitchell, Sherri. *Sacred Instructions: Indigenous Wisdom for Living Spirit-Based Change*. Berkeley: North Atlantic Books, 2018.

O'Reilley, Mary Rose. *The Peaceable Classroom*. Portsmouth, NH: Boynton/Cook, 1993.

Rendón, Laura I. *Sentipensante (Sensing/Thinking) Pedagogy: Education for Wholeness, Social Justice, and Liberation*. Sterling, VA: Stylus, 2009.

Sandoval, Chela. *Methodology of the Oppressed*. Minneapolis: University of Minnesota Press, 2000.

Smith, Linda Tuhiwai. *Decolonizing Methodologies: Research and Indigenous Peoples*. 2nd ed. London: Zed Books, 2012.

Theuring, Ashely. "Holding Hope and Doubt: An Interreligious Theopoetic Response to Public Tragedies." *Cross Currents* 4, no. 64 (2014): 549–64.

Part 3

INTERLOCUTORS

7

Imaging Loss and Longing

Doris Salcedo's Art and the Power of Collective Testimony

YOHANA AGRA JUNKER

Some of the most poignant art produced in South America from the latter half of the twentieth century to the present has been committed to imaging loss and longing while denouncing totalitarian regimes. This compendium of visual productions is one of the most powerful grounds upon which to confront the rise of dictatorships, political violence, and oppression in the region. Much of this denunciatory work invites viewers to engage with loss and longing and move into action via the aesth/ethic. Along with activists, academics, writers, and theologians, South American artists continue to resist the "wounding caused by the dehumanizing, fragmenting effects" of the colonization of the Americas.[1] By providing escape routes via the poetic, they expand our possibilities for action in order to imagine new ways of being and becoming, even in the face of impossibility. In doing so, they have revealed how these processes of wounding have marked our collective bodies. They have responded to the question posed by Pérez of how one returns from being a victim of violence, being "violated, betrayed, wounded—individually, socially, culturally, historically—with a game plan for social justice."[2] Through their work, they have condemned the derealization of our humanity, the effects of asymmetrical power relations, the rise of totalitarian regimes funded by the United States,

1. Laura E. Pérez, *Eros and Ideologies* (Durham, NC: Duke University Press, 2019), xvii.
2. Pérez, *Eros and Ideologies*, 19.

dictatorships, fascism, and the impact of economic systems that violate and subjugate populations, all while creating a public space for civic articulation and action. In this chapter, I examine the artworks of Colombian artist Doris Salcedo, highlighting how she creates poetic spaces for collective testimony. Even in the face of impossibility, violence, and dehumanization, hers is a praxis of theopoetics that reinserts forgotten bodies, narratives, and memories into public discourses through acts of witnessing, mourning, and praying. Salcedo's works maintain continuity with much of the art and theologies of liberation that emerged in South America in the '60s, '70s, and '80s. By publicly exposing the disruption and trauma caused by these systems, Salcedo's career has opened space, time and again, for collective grief to emerge, opening fissures in colonial structures. Describing her praxis as a poetics of mourning—a silent prayer—Salcedo's public art delineates what theopoet Rubem Alves names in one of his writings as the sacred: a space where humanity can cry, heal, and find respite together.[3]

MEMORIAL AESTHETICS AND THE HEALING OF WOUNDS

Public contemporary art has functioned as sites capable of shaping cultural, historical, and civic memory. A variety of artworks erected through public funding have tended to document—and often honor—colonial occupation, conquest, and war.[4] A handful of memorial artworks, however, move against monumentality, inviting participants to reflect, resist, witness, grieve, and move into the realms of emergence and possibility. These countermonuments provide viewers opportunities to confront the pain, remember the losses, name the unnamed, and experience emotions such as rage and grief *ex profundis*. Artworks that hold such tensions allow, as Devin Zuber argues, for aesthetic experiences of irresolution, openness, and uncertainty despite the tragedy the

3. Rubem Alves, *O retorno e terno*, 29th ed. (Campinas, São Paulo: Editora Papirus, 2016), 48.
4. This discussion is informed by two important essays on the status of the memorial and the aesthetic encounter with public artworks for remembrance. One is Marita Sturken's "The Wall, the Screen, and the Image: The Vietnam Veteran's Memorial," in "Monumental Histories," special issue, *Representations* 35 (Summer 1991): 118–38. Devin Zuber's essay "Flânerie at Ground Zero: Aesthetic Countermemories in Lower Manhattan," *American Quarterly* 58, no. 2 (2006): 269–99, is instrumental in my understanding of how ruins turn into political arenas and how memorial sites have continued to be highly contested in the United States, particularly after 9/11.

work memorializes.⁵ Doris Salcedo, born in Bogotá, Colombia, in 1958, is no stranger to such deep probing. The contour of human suffering is precisely what imbues her work as she coweaves with her audience threads of memorialization, presence, and visibility that resist forgetfulness. Instead of presenting an aesthetic of remedial beauty—or even representing violence explicitly—Salcedo's massive sculptures put forward the discrete—yet haunting—delineations of violence, displacement, and disenfranchisement. Found garments of those who are no longer among us, wooden chests, chairs, tables, metal rods, bricks, candles, petals, and organic elements, such as human hair, plants, and bones, are carefully assembled to construct a grammar of loss and longing.

Brazilian theologian, psychoanalyst, storyteller, and theopoet Rubem Alves has written extensively on the poetics of longing. In his *Me perguntaram se acredito em Deus (They Asked Me if I Believe in God)*, Alves describes a particular kind of longing, *saudade*, that can be translated from Portuguese as a longing that yearns to be named, felt, and remembered. This longing, which is also an aching of the soul, can be felt when profound love and irreversible absence or loss meet. To him, artistic expressions are languages that reconstruct a way forward even in the face of unfathomable pain, void, and impossibility.⁶ He writes, "*Saudade* is the presence of the absence of things we once loved but were stolen from us. . . . God exists to cure us from this *saudade*."⁷ To him, theopoetics emerges at the crossroads where bodies, desires, silent interrogations, and loss meet. In *Variaçoes sobre a vida e a morte (Variations on Life and Death)* he writes

> Theology is a way of speaking about bodies
> The bodies of those who have been sacrificed.
> The Bodies that pronounce a sacred name:
> God. . . .⁸

To Alves, theologians and artists animate symbols and coweave a poetic tapestry wide enough to cast itself over our abysses so we can attempt to traverse them.⁹ In some ways, Salcedo achieves that in her monuments—she creates a

5. Zuber, "Flânerie at Ground Zero," 296.
6. Rubem Alves, *Me perguntaram se acredito em Deus*, 2nd ed. (Campinas, São Paulo: Editora Planeta, 2013), 7.
7. Alves, *Me perguntaram*, 55.
8. Rubem Alves, *Variações sobre a vida e a morte*, 3rd ed. (Campinas, São Paulo: Edições Paulinas, 1982), 13.
9. Alves, *Variações*, 27.

tapestry full of symbolic objects that help those who experience loss cross the abyss created by colonial violence, absence, and longing.

In *Noviembre 6 y 7* (staged in 2002), for example, she constructed a momentary memorial to the 1985 victims of the siege of the *Palacio de Justicia* in Bogotá. On this occasion, victims were held hostage by a guerrilla group in a process that lasted fifty-three hours and killed 284 persons inside the palace. Through the artwork, Salcedo reproduced the duration and magnitude of the siege by lowering 284 empty chairs from the top of the Palace of Justice's facade on the seventeenth anniversary of the seizure. Starting at exactly 11:35 a.m. on November 6, 2002, Salcedo marked the tempo at which each victim was shot. The empty chairs, she explains, "are statements of absence allowing one to be aware of the fragility of those who were behind those walls . . . [they] emphasize the vulnerability, not only of those who worked in the Palace of Justice but of us all."[10] Salcedo's accomplishment is the conversion of the forgotten into *present*, and more precisely, into a *presence*. The artist establishes an inescapable relationship between spectators-as-witnesses and the work of art. These chairs, a tapestry for crossing over such an unspeakable abyss, evoke the memory of the disappeared, the bodies that were sacrificed, turning swords into plows, as Alves puts it. Moreover, Salcedo invites those who survived to acknowledge and enunciate the pain while resisting and fashioning a way forward. In this piece, Salcedo transforms loss into symbolic presence that immortalizes, dignifies, and confers visibility to stories erased from public memory, official discourses, and a country's national history.[11] In such a ritual of public, symbolic, and tacit mourning, Salcedo remains true to her aesth/ ethic. She writes: "The only concern of my work is what happens to human beings assaulted by violence."[12] These public installations, she writes, "attempt to give back the sense, meaning, and form that violence took away from its victims, the unmourned dead of the past" (216). And this particular work did, indeed, move the audience to witness such silent, public ritual in a state of reverence, achieving yet another aim of the artist: "to inscribe a different kind of passage, that is, from suffering to signifying loss" (215). As one critic wrote, the result of these performances is immeasurable: "If mourning restores

10. Doris Salcedo, "Proposal for a Project for the Palace of Justice, Bogotá, 2002," in *Doris Salcedo: Shibboleth*, ed. Achim Borchardt-Hume (London: Tate, 2007), 83.

11. Lori Cole, "At the Site of State Violence: Doris Salcedo's and Julieta Hanono's Memorial Aesthetics," *Arizona Journal of Hispanic Cultural Studies* 15 (2001): 87–93.

12. Julie Rodrigues Widholm and Madeleine Grynsztejn, eds., *Doris Salcedo* (Chicago: Museum of Contemporary Art Chicago, 2015), 215. Hereafter, references to this source will appear in the text.

humanity, and Salcedo's sculptures create sites for mourning, then she creates art that counters dehumanizing acts with humane ones" (19). Echoing the words of Rubem Alves, Salcedo determines that her artworks move beyond the violence. They configure mourning rituals, funeral orations, and an encounter that "is both a confrontation and an embrace" (216).

ART AS RITUAL AND COLLECTIVE TESTIMONY

Acción de duelo also functioned as a "solitary liturgy" for lament, as one critic once wrote (212). Staged in 2007, and four days after the announcement that FARC (Revolutionary Armed Forces in Colombia) had murdered eleven members of the Parliament who had been held hostage for five years, Salcedo placed twenty-four thousand votive candles in the open Plaza de Bolívar, in Bogotá. Bearing witness to the lives and loves lost to state violence in Colombia, she lit each candle, delineating a solitary liturgy of lament. As hundreds of people gathered to witness her ritual, they became implicated in the act. They were moved to join her in honoring lost lives by lighting one candle at a time, symbolically weaving a sacred web over such void. This staging was a mandate to communally put in motion acts that confront, expose, and lament the compounding effects of the brutal losses. To Rubem Alves, poetic gestures such as these are fundamental in communities that endure trauma, genocide, "enslavement, desertedness, exile, devastation, and foreign [political] domination."[13] Speaking from his own experience, Alves was no stranger to the turmoil and anguish instituted by totalitarian regimes. In his *Por uma educação romantica* (*Toward a Romantic Education*), Alves discloses what it felt like to wake up on March 31, 1964, with the news of the coup that gave rise to the harrowing military dictatorship in Brazil. At the time, Alves was finishing a master's degree in New York, and upon returning to Brazil the following year, he felt as though he was "standing before an abyss."[14] His friends informed him that he was on the military's Supreme Council "wanted list" with more than forty accusations to his name. Going into exile was the only viable option for him and his family, and Princeton Theological Seminary became home for them. Loss and longing, saudade and lament became his language during his exile years. And, just as *Acción de duelo* became Salcedo's silent liturgies, Alves's theopoetics and writing were drenched with invocations, evocations, and longings of hope. "Isn't every

13. Alves, *Variações*, 137.
14. Rubem Alves, *Por uma educação romântica* (Campinas, SP: Papirus, 2012), 16–17.

liturgy," he asks, "a choreography that dances to the sound of the song that is born from an absence?"[15] As each person was compelled to help Salcedo light thousands of candles in *Acción de duelo*, a community emerged to inspire and conspire together, drawing into light one absent life at a time.

In the same year of this public mourning ritual, Salcedo conjured a monumental achievement at the Tate Modern's Turbine Hall: she created a direct chasm on the floor of one of the museum's most celebrated halls through a work entitled *Shibboleth*. Salcedo's explicit subversion of monumentality directs the viewer's experience to a 167-meter crack that runs the length of the gallery. By making the floor and viewers' bodies the focus of this countersculpture, absence is made present through a fissure that demands from viewers both reflection and a crossing over. As Elizabeth Adan puts it, "Salcedo used space to foreground populations subjected to various state forces, along with mechanisms of power that sustain such forces by transforming prominent Western galleries and museums into sites of separation."[16] As the spectator stands before such scar tissue—or attempts to traverse it—they cannot dismiss themes of division, segregation, and naturalized oppression. Salcedo explains:

> I am making a piece about people who have been subject to inhumane conditions in the first world. It is trying to introduce into Turbine Hall another perspective. . . . It's a piece that is both in the epicenter of catastrophe and outside the catastrophe. I wanted a piece that intruded in the space, like an immigrant, a presence that questions the foundations upon Western notions of modernity are built. . . . Once the show is over, the piece will be sealed so a permanent scar will always be in the Turbine Hall as a commemoration of all this life we don't want to see. The presence of the life we don't want to acknowledge will be there forever.[17]

Salcedo chose to name the work *Shibboleth* as a direct reference to the book of Judges, where Ephraimites attempted to cross the Jordan to escape. Gilead soldiers could identify those on the run by asking them to pronounce the word Shibboleth. Since Ephraimites could not pronounce the "sh" sound, a massacre ensued. The biblical text says that forty-two thousand people were killed. "I use this word to refer to the experience of racism, crossing borders, the experience

15. Alves, *Variações*, 139.
16. Widholm and Grynsztej, *Doris Salcedo*, 36.
17. Salcedo in an interview with Tate Modern's *TateShots*. It can be viewed at Doris Salcedo *Shibboleth*, The Unilever Series, October 9, 2007, through April 6, 2008, Tate Modern Turbine Hall, https://www.youtube.com/watch?v=NIJDn2MAn9I. Last accessed January 17, 2023.

of the immigrant, what it means to die in an attempt of crossing a border."[18] The embodied experience of traversing the topography of the Turbine Hall grows viscerally as the participants walk through the hall. The beginning of the crack is quite small, imperceptible, and superficial. However, it widens and deepens as it reaches the other side of the gallery. By activating our bodies, memories, and visceral responses to the sculpture, Salcedo once again stages a collective witnessing of absences and longings, the violence of erasure and exclusion, and the horror that breathes in our condoned practices of cruelty, as Alves reminds us.[19] As Catherine Keller points out, this capacity to "speak truth—sometimes to power, sometimes to the disempowered—is what in the religious traditions we mean by "witness" or "testimony.""[20] Salcedo engages with theopoetics when she invites us to touch such human fissures in hopes that a way forward may be opened where there had been none. By making our fractures visible, she releases the possibility of creating a reality "across and beyond disaster."[21] Though monumental in scale, her installations evoke intimacy. She explains:

> I want to make private pain into something public because it is not a private problem, it is a public problem. . . . My work is based not on my experience but on somebody else's experience. . . . Experience means going across danger. . . . I come from Colombia, a country where there's nothing but ruins. That's what wars, imperialism, colonialism left us. . . . From the perspective of the victim . . . it's where I'm seeing, I'm looking at the world. So I am trying to rescue that memory. . . . My work . . . [is] a hint of something. It is trying to bring into our presence something that is no longer here. . . . It was the height of the paramilitary massacres in Colombia. It was my way of showing how life could be wasted but at the same time you could build something that was poetic that could give testimony to human presence and to the humanness of these victims and the fragility of life and the brutality of power. . . . I want to make private pain into something public because it is not a private problem; it is a public problem.[22]

Taken together, these site-specific and momentary installations invite us to inhabit the tenuous space of collective testimony. As people are drawn to

18. Doris Salcedo, "Compassion," season five of *Art in the Twenty-First Century*, https://art21.org/watch/art-in-the-twenty-first-century/s5/doris-salcedo-in-compassion-segment/, last accessed January 17, 2023.

19. Rubem Alves, *I Believe in the Resurrection of the Body* (Eugene, OR: Wipf & Stock, 1986), 68.

20. Catherine Keller, *Discerning Divinity in the Process* (Minneapolis: Fortress, 2007), 28.

21. Widholm and Grynsztejn, *Doris Salcedo*, 217.

22. Salcedo, "Compassion."

witness the lowering of the chairs, light candles across plazas, follow a fissure on a museum's gallery, Salcedo invites us to mourn, lament, and traverse a *via crucis*. Tensions, questions, and longings saturate these journeys. Can life continue to be affirmed as poetic and beautiful despite unutterable loss? Can one transmute the incontestable sepulchral character of the artist's composition to affirm life at the other end of the hall, the ritual, the witness? Mayra Rivera's *The Poetics of the Flesh* offers a poignant reflection on how Christians have understood carnal relationships within the world.[23] Drawing on the writings of Rubem Alves and Merleau-Ponty's "corporeal schema," she writes: "God's desire to be a body inspires [Rubem Alves's] celebration of corporeality—of human compassion, gardens, and poetry. He calls his readers to remember the Christian dogma to renew their commitments to justice and hope."[24] Works such as *Shibboleth* and *Acción de duelo* have moved bodies to converge with histories, memories, stories, and spaces, requiring witnesses to sit in reverence before countless losses and longings. With this grammar of sensing, seeing, and lamenting, Salcedo activates both the sensorial and the memorial realms, asking us to mobilize and envision life otherwise. Marked within these sculptures, assemblages, and collective testimony is a renewed commitment toward justice and hope, as Rivera remarked. As bodies assemble to witness, perform, mourn, and resist woundedness out in the open, they develop tools to contest and undo modes of violent abuse, precarity, and control. As Judith Butler expands,

> Only when bodies assemble on the street, in the square, or in other forms of public space (including virtual ones) they are exercising a plural and performative right to appear, one that asserts and instates the body in the midst of the political field, and which, in its expressive and signifying function delivers a bodily demand for a more livable set of economic, social, and political conditions no longer afflicted by induced forms of precarity.[25]

Such assemblies, processions, and memorial witnessing give way to a collective demand for a more livable life. A life that acknowledges and names the stories, trajectories, desires, and yearnings of those who are no longer here with us. In some ways, Salcedo's poetics of mourning reverberate with traces

---

23. Mayra Rivera, *Poetics of the Flesh* (Durham, NC: Duke University Press, 2015).
24. Rivera, *Poetics of the Flesh*, 59.
25. Judith Butler, *Notes Toward a Performative Theory of Assembly* (Cambridge: Harvard University Press, 2015), 11.

of a story Rubem Alves told about his early years in Dores da Boa Esperança. "When I was a child in my hometown," he recounts, "when people passed away, all the churches would ring their memorial bells. Everyone knew that, somewhere in our town, people were crying. And a sacred space would crack open. After all, what are sacred spaces if not a place where humanity can cry together?"[26] Marking a breakthrough in contemporary art, Salcedo's works resist a culture of erasure and collective amnesia. Her art defies forgetfulness and resounds bells that remind us that, somewhere in our town, people are crying. Salcedo's art stages, time and again, outbursts of history, bodies, memory, and remembrances that emerge from the grounds of our societal and psychic structures to become memorialized, even if just fleetingly. Through her theopoetics, we re-member the power of collective testimony to coweave poetic and imaginative webs over woundedness and abysses.

Works Cited

Alves, Rubem. *I Believe in the Resurrection of the Body*. Eugene, OR: Wipf & Stock, 1986.

———. *Me perguntaram se acredito em Deus*. 2nd ed. Campinas, São Paulo: Editora Planeta, 2013.

———. *O retorno e terno*. 29th ed. Campinas, São Paulo: Editora Papirus, 2016.

———. *Por uma educação romântica*. Campinas, São Paulo: Papirus, 2012.

———. *Variações sobre a vida e a morte*. 3rd ed. Campinas, São Paulo: Edições Paulinas, 1982.

Butler, Judith. *Notes Toward a Performative Theory of Assembly*. Cambridge: Harvard University Press, 2015.

Cole, Lori. "At the Site of State Violence: Doris Salcedo's and Julieta Hanono's Memorial Aesthetics." *Arizona Journal of Hispanic Cultural Studies* 15 (2001): 87–93.

Keller, Catherine. *Discerning Divinity in the Process*. Minneapolis: Fortress, 2007.

Pérez, Laura E. *Eros and Ideologies*. Durham, NC: Duke University Press, 2019.

Rivera, Mayra. *Poetics of the Flesh*. Durham, NC: Duke University Press, 2015.

Salcedo, Doris. "Compassion." Season five of *Art in the Twenty-First Century*, https://art21.org/watch/art-in-the-twenty-first-century/s5/doris-salcedo -in-compassion-segment/, last accessed January 17, 2023.

---

26. Alves, *O Retorno e Terno*, 48.

———. "Proposal for a Project for the Palace of Justice, Bogotá, 2002." In *Doris Salcedo: Shibboleth*, edited by Achim Borchardt-Hume, 83. London: Tate, 2007.

———. *Shibboleth*. The Unilever Series, October 9, 2007, through April 6, 2008. Tate Modern Turbine Hall. https://www.youtube.com/watch?v=NIJDn2MAn9I. Last accessed, January 17, 2023.

Sturken, Marita. "The Wall, the Screen, and the Image: The Vietnam Veteran's Memorial." In "Monumental Histories." Special issue, *Representations* 35 (1991): 118–38.

Widholm, Julie Rodrigues, and Madeleine Grynsztejn, eds. *Doris Salcedo*. Chicago: Museum of Contemporary Art Chicago, 2015.

Zuber, Devin. "Flânerie at Ground Zero: Aesthetic Countermemories in Lower Manhattan." *American Quarterly* 58, no. 2 (2006): 269–99.

8

Somethin' Like Sanctified

Theopoetics, Black Music, and the Strangeness of Estrangement

JAMES HOWARD HILL JR.

*The following chapter engages explicit themes of intimate family violence. Reader's discretion is advised.

There is nothing rational about intimate family violence. It is no coincidence that few—if any—theologies (or works indexed within the genre "theopoetics") are explicitly written from the perspective of Black men who carry the consequences of intimate family violence within our bodies. An untold number of Black boys and Black men struggle in secret to reconcile the God our fathers taught us with the violence, fear, instability, and shame our fathers gave us. Within our bodies, we carry a particular theodicy few (if any) seminaries care to help us resolve: How can a loving God place their Spirit within the bruised bodies of our mamas? How can a loving God who "sits high and looks low" not protect our mamas from the wrath of our fathers? We struggle to forgive ourselves for loving the same men who made us feel like cowards for not being able to protect our spirit-filled mamas. What good is a theopoetics that offers nothing to the Black boys who grew up to be Black men haunted by a shame that was never ours to carry? What relevance does theopoetics hold for the Black boys and Black men who carry within ourselves the penalty of not protecting our mothers from the men who look and laugh like us? The following words and writerly experimentations are dedicated to everyone—especially the Black boys and men—whose relationship to spirituality, with religious speech and life-writing is fused to a groaning too deep for words that reside within the catacombs of our haunted and haunting Black lives. I love you all.

There's Nothing Wrong with Me Loving You

I can clearly recall the first time I saw my dad cry.

He was sitting atop the toilet seat, fully clothed, head buried in his hands.

"Dad, what's wrong?" I remember asking him as I crossed the bathroom threshold.

"Just go away," he replied through tears.

"No, don't go away," I countered with an innocence that was as soft as it was unknowing.

An argument between my dad and my mother occasioned the opportunity for the two of us to have our first misunderstanding. My only other memory from that encounter is climbing into my dad's lap in an attempt to both offer solace and relocate my resting place. While I have little desire to define theopoetics personally, I can say that whatever relationship I have to poetics, God, and life itself was first formed within the tear-soaked interstices of my dad's broken embrace.

In a 1993 interview with Oprah Winfrey that ninety million people viewed, Michael Jackson talked openly for the first time about his father, Joe Jackson. "I love my father, but I do not know him," Michael shared with Oprah and the world. A few moments later, Michael would vulnerably confess that Joe Jackson's opacity and willful unknowability caused his son, the King of Pop, to sometimes become angry. Black popular music, among other things, is textured by the haunted (and haunting) relationship between Black men and our Black fathers. Far too often, the complicated relationship between Black men and our fathers has been weaponized and deployed upon Black women in order to signify them as, somehow, being inherently inadequate, incomplete, and unfit to raise Black boys. This is bullshit. While our mothers are indelibly woven into the fabric of our relationship with our fathers (whether they desired to be or not is an entirely different conversation), reducing them to villains, foils, or hapless, inert victims of white supremacism is the epitome of cowardice. Such cowardice emerges from the simple fact that, far too often, Black fathers and Black sons are too haunted to behold one another in the indicting and healing light of truth.

WE'RE ALL SENSITIVE PEOPLE

I can clearly recall the second time I saw my dad cry.

We were in Anniston, Alabama, visiting my aunt Johnnie-Mae. A devoutly Christian woman, Aunt Johnnie-Mae beamed with pride on Sunday morning as she showed us off to her church family. During the altar call portion of the Sunday morning service, I watched my dad get down on both knees and bend so low that I would not be surprised if his forehead found temporary reprieve in the sanctuary carpet. Once the minister brought the prayer to a close, I saw my dad arise, eyes bloodshot, cheeks filled with tears, mustache matted with holy snot. He quietly took his handkerchief out of his blazer pocket and wiped his face as he sat down quietly beside Aunt Johnnie-Mae and our family.

Upon conclusion of the service, Aunt Johnnie-Mae proudly ushered us to the front of the church so we could meet her pastor. After shaking our hands, the pastor looked intently into the tear-stained countenance of my dad and began to prophesy to him on the spot. While I do not remember the contents of the prophecy itself, I do remember the pastor telling my dad that he was "in need of a father" and that he would step into the gap and become a father for him. Upon hearing these words spoken over him at the altar, my dad broke down and became an amalgamation of mucous, tears, and all the unreconciled childhood pain that his beautiful Black body was tired of holding. As I looked up at my dad, my nine-year-old mind could not help but think, "Does the preacher know Dad doesn't have a dad?" Ultimately, that question did not matter because that was the last time we would ever see or hear from Aunt Johnnie-Mae's pastor.

Scenes of my dad weeping in a church service did not unnerve me. I grew up to the sounds of my dad—an ordained Baptist minister in his own right—singing gospel classics like "In Times Like These," "My Soul Has Been Anchored," and "I Won't Complain." He often sang these songs in the kitchen as he cooked one of his patented "Daddy Hill" breakfast meals. Whether breakfast or dinner meals, Daddy Hill's care-full cooking earned him instant praise and love by anyone fortunate enough to touch one of his prepared plates. On more than a few occasions, I delighted in peeking around the corner and staring in stealth, holy wonder as my dad hummed over a running faucet a melody that I'm sure caused the angels in heaven to rededicate their lives. To this day, I am not sure if our dirty dishes were cleaned by Dawn or my Daddy Hill's gospel-textured tears.

James Howard Hill Jr.

DON'T YOU KNOW HOW SWEET AND WONDERFUL LIFE CAN BE?

I can clearly recall the third time I saw my father cry.

By the time I was sixteen, I carried within my teenage Black body the memories and hauntings of all the arguments between my father and mother that quickly spiraled into violence. These hauntings codified the images, sounds, and abject terror of witnessing my father assault my mother. Whether it was the stairs or the kitchen, bedrooms or our carport, there was no inch of our home that did not double as haunting sites of family violence.

By the time I was sixteen, I considered my father to be many things, but a hero was not one of them. Besides the wrath he unleashed on my mother when he was under the influence of drugs and alcohol, he grew to signify, for me, a walking hypocrisy that was as infuriating as it was disappointing. If the disease of addiction ever destroyed a family, it destroyed mine. In 2004, few Black children in my neighborhood had the intellectual scaffolding necessary to account for how addiction was a disease often tethered to comorbid mental health challenges and not a moral failing rooted in our parent's lack of will. As a teenager, I had no tools to hold within me the fact that my father was a Black man who experienced childhood trauma so severe he will likely conceal it within himself all the way to the grave. No one provided me with the skills to hold space and mourn the fact that the teenage version of my father was molded into a sailor immediately after his high school graduation and thrust into the Vietnam War during the Fall of Saigon. Regrettably, I saw him only as an abuser, a coward, a soulless villain unfit to bear the title "Dad."

My eroding confidence in my father's character—and his God—compelled me to find heroes and interlocutors within the domain of popular culture. Because I attended four elementary schools in six years and three high schools in four years, I did not have the type of friendships that a grounded, stable childhood provided. In need of friendship, mentorship, and spiritual formation, I turned to the music of Black men who, in one way or another, reflected my trauma-informed Black teenage life back to me. First on my list of Black male celebrity interlocutors was none other than Michael Joe Jackson. Michael was the first person who "taught" me that abused Black boys could still produce magic. Tragically, Michael would later teach me the depths to which magic cannot conceal Black-boy horror or its haunting afterlives. Next was JAY-Z. Hov taught me that there was no single aspect of a Black boy's life that a Black boy's pen could not touch. JAY-Z's eighth studio album, *The Black Album*, was released during my sophomore year in high school. "December 4th," the second track on the album, was the first song that moved me to tears. Up to that moment, I had never read or listened to poetry written by a Black man that narrated the traumatic experiences of sensitive Black boys haunted by the refusal of our fathers to lead us, love us, and fight for us.

Marvin Gaye was the third artist in my triumvirate of sensitive Black men. Though I admittedly did not know a great amount concerning the details of Marvin's challenging life, I knew that he sang about God in his music and that his father was a minister who killed him. That was enough for this sixteen-year-old son of a tortured Baptist minister to name Marvin an interlocutor and add his sonic oeuvre to my other study materials.

On one particular night, my study session with Marvin was interrupted by a knock on the door. I instantly knew that it was my father on the other side. My parents typically could not go ninety days without yelling at the top of their lungs about what they hated about each other. Sometimes my brother and I got front-row seats to the show. Other times, I awoke in the middle of the night to murmurs that soon became high-pitched shrills and expletive-laden name-calling. This evening was one of the more quotidian arguments. No physical altercations. No red and blue police lights accenting our windows. Just yelling and the typical barrage of "I hate you!" that my brother and I learned to drown out with music.

While I was used to my parents arguing, I was not used to any of them knocking on our doors immediately afterward. "Come in," I said to my father in a tone that was even parts anxious, confused, and curious. The man who walked into the room was not the authoritarian I was expecting. This man looked defeated and bereft of even the faintest semblance of hope or belief in himself. He sat on the edge of my bed with slumped shoulders and looked at me with eyes heavy from tears and weariness.

"I just wanted to apologize to you, June," my dad began. Now he had my attention.

"Your dad is a screw up, man. I'm sorry. I keep messing up, and I'm sorry you have to see this. Be a better man than me, son." As he struggled to bring the last sentence to a close, his levy broke. Tears began to stream down his face. Snot once again took residence above his upper lip. Each breath of his became more labored as he struggled to contain the tears and snot that spoke of a love that speech no longer communicated.

As I looked at my father, every ounce of my sixteen-year-old body wanted to climb into his tear-soaked lap and relocate the resting place drugs, alcohol, and foolish pride took away from me. I wanted to hold my father and tell him to come back to us. I wanted to remind him of the songs he used to sing over fluffy scrambled eggs and Jimmy Dean breakfast sausage patties. I wanted to tell him that I missed my friend, the dad who spent entire afternoons arranging my Ninja Turtles action figures beneath the sound of his son's soft command. I wanted to tell him that nothing could separate me from loving him, not drugs, not alcohol, not even the violence we were forced to absorb and internalize. I wanted to tell him that I was committed to holding onto the name he gave me until it signified everything he could not. I wanted, more than anything else, to put the pieces of my father back together and tell him that I loved him.

"OK," I said.

My dad took a few seconds to collect himself, wiped his nose with the sleeve of his shirt, kissed me on my forehead, told me he loved me, and walked out of my room to give a version of the same apology to my younger brother. Once the door closed, I turned Marvin back on—and cried myself to sleep.

SINCE WE GOT TO BE HERE, LET'S LIVE (I LOVE YOU)

On April 1, 1984, at 12:38 p.m., Marvin Pentz Gay Jr. was shot and killed by his father, Minister Marvin Gay Sr. This tragic act of paternal filicide immediately sent shockwaves throughout popular culture that quickly spread throughout the world. Fans, critics, and family members would recall Marvin's open struggle to see himself beyond the pained witness of his childhood self. A survivor of corporal punishment, Marvin spent much of his life struggling to reconcile his indefatigable love of God with a life that was formed within the crucible of an unknowable Black father. While many Black children grew up hearing a version of "I brought you into this world, and I will take you out!" Marvin Jr. and Marvin Sr. dramatized the death-dealing consequences of dismissing such statements as rhetorically effective displays of "tough love."

While Marvin Jr. knew his father's God, he never knew his father. Within the death-bound tragedy dramatized by Marvin Jr. and Marvin Sr., we find examples of drug abuse, depression, violence, a weeping mother who refused comfort, Christian piety, worship, love, and fear. However, the violent relationship between Marvin Jr. and Marvin Sr. is far more than an unfortunate account of a violent father who could not summon the means to love his troubled son. At the heart of the Gay family story is an account of shame, of a love refused, of Black men who were not free to live, love, and be who they are in the light of truth. Marvin Sr. openly wore women's clothing and carried within his anointed Black body the significations of the sissy. His father's unwillingness to perform proper masculine conduct caused young Marvin Jr. to become a target of incessant bullying from his peers. The Black queer antagonism Marvin faced as a child would be a critical factor in his decision to add an *e* to his last name once he became famous.

Unlike Marvin, I never added anything to my name to conceal the lingering reminders of past trouble. However, like Marvin, I, too, am a Jr. who turned to the God of my minister father for rest and escape. I know all too well the consequences of being reared in the shadow of a sanctified contradiction. My father never wore my mother's clothes, nor did he give neighborhood kids a reason to question his—or my—sexuality. However, the things I found and observed within my home caused me to struggle to love God, my body, and the embrace of every lover who considered it not robbery to touch me until shame was no longer my portion. Like Marvin and Michael, I turned to the poetics found within theology and the Bible upon discovering that I no longer fit within my dad's broken embrace.

My parents divorced when I was eighteen. By that time, my father and I had little semblance of a relationship. Over the next several years we attempted to fight the good fight. He called me on most birthdays. I worked hard to overcome my anxiety and call him every Father's Day. My wife and I even made several trips to visit him at his new home. But, for all intents and purposes, there was little left between us. By the spring of 2020, the only thing of my father's that I still had in my possession was his name, his pain, his music, and the God he gave me.

Within this paradigm, theopoetics, the poetics of a life-writing haunted by what the Greek tragedian Aeschylus termed "the awful grace of God," provides an occasion to attend to a groaning too deep for words. No account of divine poetics is complete without an account of the ways God-speech and God-writing guides us through the visceral strangeness of estrangement. My father taught me that it was OK for Black boys to cry—only to leave me to myself and my tears. The same man whose pulpit presence and heavenly voice ushered me into the life I live now is not a part of my children's world. I know the response from many is to seek reconciliation one more time. Endure the pain of rejection. Learn to absorb the deregulated emotions, toxic communication, and flagrant unrepentant posture toward the past and present. While this may be standard Christian practice, Christians must face the fact that we have sent far too many children back into the arms of parents who had no intention of loving them in a manner worthy of their witness.

Theopoetics, for me, does not require a false declaration of "Peace, Peace!" when we know there will never be peace. Theopoetics does not require any of us to use language in service of our humiliation. Theopoetics, instead, provides us with a method to sit in the room with our ghosts, our hauntings, ourselves—and wait awhile. Theopoetics provides a way to account for a spirituality that demands us to interrogate it perpetually if we ever desire to live into it fully. Theopoetics is the chosen mode of language I use to remind God and myself that, despite myself, I am only able to love because my father first loved me.

I love my father, but I do not know him.
I love my father, but I do not know him.
I love my father, but I do not know him.
I love my father, but I do not know him.
I love my father, but I do not know him.
I love my Father,
but I do not know Him.

9

"In the Dark, We Can All Be Free"

The Sacralizing Vision of Alvin Baltrop

PEACE PYUNGHWA LEE

*Untitled (Sunbathers) (c. 1975–86) by Alvin Baltrop, © 2023 Estate of Alvin Baltrop /
Artists Rights Society (ARS), New York*

The title of this chapter comes from Valerie Cassel Oliver, "Alvin Baltrop: Dreams into
Glass," in *Alvin Baltrop: Dreams into Glass*, by Alvin Baltrop, ed. Valerie Cassel Oliver,
Perspectives 179 (Houston: Contemporary Arts Museum, 2012), 36.

I first came across Alvin Baltrop's photography at the Museum of Modern Art Public School One's (MoMA PS1) *Greater New York* exhibit in the fall of 2015. I held my breath as I took in scene after scene of naked bodies entwined in embrace or in serene repose atop ruins and decaying piers. I marveled at the easy grace of their nakedness. "They are naked and without shame" might have escaped my lips. I was drawn into what American cultural theorist Saidiya Hartman describes as the "terrible beauty" of another world evoked through Baltrop's vision.[1] I was amazed at the expressions of love and togetherness that flourished in the ruins. I was not prepared to be flooded with submerged memories from my own childhood as I lingered in the gallery. And as I reflect on Baltrop's photography now, I recognize that he is witnessing to "a wild place that is not simply the leftover space that limns real and regulated zones of polite society" but "a wild place that continuously produces its own unregulated wildness" as it reminds us of a world that has been, is already here, ours for the taking and for creating.[2]

A Walk through the Terrible Beauty of a Manilan Slum

I can still visualize the throng of stark-naked children from my childhood memories, their chocolate bodies glistening with rain. A rumble in the sky was enough to draw a swarm of Filipino children outside into the courtyard of a shabby apartment complex in Manila. That was the cue for me to take my seat on the balcony and watch their congregation. As water poured from the heavens, children cast off their clothes howling in delight. A bar of soap was passed around and dutifully used, but it was the shampoo bottle that was squeezed lavishly, extravagantly, atop heads but also chests and thighs. The children would rub themselves and sometimes each other until frothy bubbles bloomed forth from their touches. They would flick and blow and smear the bubbles on each other's faces and bottoms as they chased each other until all traces of soap was washed away.

I always wanted to join in the sound of children trilling with laughter and dancing about under the rush of rain. I longed to strip off my sticky clothes

---

1. Saidiya Hartman, "The Terrible Beauty of the Slum," *Brick: A Literary Journal*, July 28, 2017, https://brickmag.com/the-terrible-beauty-of-the-slum/.

2. Jack Halberstam, "The Wild Beyond: With and for the Undercommons," in *The Undercommons: Fugitive Planning & Black Study*, by Stefano Harney and Fred Moten (New York: Minor Composition, 2013), 7.

that clung and chafed against my heat-rashed back and feel the balm of rainwater on my skin. I wanted to dance in the rain singing and laughing. But when I asked my parents if I could join the other children and shower in the rain, I was met with, "Do you want to go bald from acid rain? Don't you know it's a shame to run around naked?" Only after the rain stopped and the spectacle of naked children departed was I allowed outside. I would dip my foot into the shallow rainbow-ringed pools left behind by laughing children whose heads were full of hair.

I never knew any of the children, though I came to recognize some of their bodies better than my own. I remember a girl with a penny-sized mole on her neck that gleamed like a dark pearl. I also recall the thrill of recognition when I made out a blue Mongolian spot on the butt of a caramel-colored Filipino boy. I remember wanting to cast off my shirt and point to the bluish smudge on my stomach and say to him, "Look! See this? This means we're related." But I could not join in when he was dancing, baring his fluttering Mongolian watermark.

I did not know any of the local children in my neighborhood because I went to a private Christian school for missionary children. It also did not help that our run-down neighborhood did not have a playground or a park. Only an abandoned swimming pool, long turned into a trash dump with rusty water, lay at the edge of our apartment complex. The color of the viscous liquid was that of blood and rust. The pool was Olympic sized, and in its cloudy water floated all sorts of things, like a bent bicycle wheel, a hollowed-out TV with a shattered screen, and shapeless stuffed animals with exploded seams. By the time I was living there, it had long turned into the town dump. Boys and even grown-up men projectile peed into the pool, aiming to hit a floating toy truck that bobbed not too far from the edge. I often quickened my steps whenever I had to pass the pool because it reeked of urine and sulfur.

But one day, I saw three caramel-colored boys strip down and dive into the pool, splashing about with delight in the dark waters. They took turns diving, their pointed toes and heels undulating above the surface. They played mimicking deep-sea divers and explorers; I fell under their spell and became a captive audience. I held my breath as each one dived deep, wondering what buried and forgotten treasure the pool might yield. A limbless robot, a tarnished costume necklace, and a headless Barbie doll were scrounged up. It was only when one of the boys broke the surface, clutching victoriously at what turned out to be a soiled diaper, that I sighed, exhaling all sense of hope. The magic of the scene that had transformed the decaying pool into an oasis of exploration evaporated as fast as my breath returned, the stench of the place hitting me afresh. I started walking away but heard echoes of gurgling laughter behind me. I felt protective when adults I knew disparaged these children, "Don't you dare play with them. They are dirtier than animals."

THE SEWER RAT IN THE SEWER

The late American photographer Alvin Baltrop was once called a "sewer rat because of the content" of his art.[3] Baltrop photographed Manhattan's Hudson River piers between 1975 and 1986, revealing a world of queer sociality that was created in the vast industrial ruins of abandoned warehouses and steel piers. Saidiya Hartman's description of the slums illuminates the ruins of Baltrop's photography as the ruins, too, are a "raucous disorderly world, a place defined by tumult, *vulgar collectivism*, and *anarchy*."[4] The ruins of the piers are indeed "wretched," a "human sewer populated by the worst elements" (Hartman). Peter Eleey, curator of MoMA PS1, reflects that "Baltrop documented the piers in disuse, during years when they were repurposed by people at the margins, for shelter, sex, and social gathering."[5]

Abandoned and thus unregulated, in the wasteland that is the piers flourished a refuge of queer sociality wherein the marginalized and the miscellany mingled in myriads of ways. Thus it is indeed a "social laboratory," "a space of encounter," an "urban commons where the poor assemble, improvise the forms of life, experiment with freedom" (Hartman). As art historian Douglas Crimp notes, in Baltrop's pictures we glimpse "how unpoliced public spaces served shared desires."[6] Baltrop recognized the revolutionary potential of such a space; he saw in the piers "spaces and modalities that exist separate from the logical, the logistical, the housed and the positioned"[7] and revealed the movements of fugitive and elusive bodies in all of its "clandestine arrangements, wayward lives, carnal matters" (Hartman) as it took shape and blossomed in the unsurveilled space of society's margins.

---

3. Osa Atoe, "Alvin Baltrop: A Queer Black Photographer's Groundbreaking Work Comes to Life Five Years after His Death," *Colorlines*, March 24, 2009, https://www.color lines.com/articles/alvin-baltrop.

4. Hartman, "Terrible Beauty of the Slum." Hereafter, references to this source will appear in the text.

5. Carl Swanson, "Manhattan's West Side Piers, Back When They Were Naked and Gay," *New York Magazine*, November 18, 2015, http://nymag.com/daily/intelligencer/2015/11/west-side-piers-when-they-were-naked-and-gay.html.

6. Douglas Crimp, preface to *Alvin Baltrop*, 11.

7. Halberstam, "Wild Beyond," 11.

Baltrop was no stranger to being overlooked or living in the margins of society. The particularity of his queer and Black body made him especially invisible and explains why his larger body of work was often excluded from the corpus of fine art photography. Baltrop struggled to find membership in the art world, facing racism and homophobia as a Black and queer person. According to Baltrop's friend and assistant Randal Wilcox, Baltrop faced "constant racism from gay curators, gallery owners and other members of the 'gay community' until his death."[8] Wilcox recounts that many "doubted that Baltrop shot his own photographs" and some even "stole photographs from him."[9] It is no surprise, then, that Baltrop's portfolio was fiercely rejected as curators condemned his work as vulgar, indecent, and unworthy to be called; one curator even called Baltrop a "sewer rat," undercutting his humanity and the humanities in his art. But Baltrop refused to be shamed into silence and oblivion. He believed that artists exist to "communicate things that would otherwise remain unseen and forgotten,"[10] and he pressed on, witnessing to the Undercommons of the piers, striving to "reshape desire, reorient hope, reimagine possibility and do so separate from the fantasies nestled into rights and respectability."[11]

Baltrop is certainly not the first to have photographed another form of life or witness to bodies and modalities that society has condemned or erased as deviant and degenerate. Photographers like Diane Arbus and her famed portraits of "freaks" as she called them have spawned endless debate about aesthetics and ethics, about art and politics. Hartman is all too aware of the exploitative gaze of the "social scientists and the reformers" who show up at the margins with their "cameras and their surveys, staring intently at all the strange specimens" (Hartman). In the case of Baltrop, however, the usual distinctions drawn between photographer and the subject dissolve. For one thing, Baltrop did not make any money from his photographs, nor did he receive fame or recognition. If anything, he poured out all that he had in terms of his resources, all of who he was, to witness to a form of life whose very existence was not just denied but actively suppressed by others. In that sense Baltrop trod the "path to the wild beyond,"[12] refusing what had been refused to him,

---

8. Wilcox in Atoe, "Alvin Baltrop."

9. Wilcox in Atoe, "Alvin Baltrop."

10. Randal Wilcox, afterword to *Alvin Baltrop: Dreams into Glass*, by Alvin Baltrop, Perspectives 179, edited by Valerie Cassel Oliver. Houston: Contemporary Arts Museum, 2012, 58.

11. Halberstam, "Wild Beyond," 12.

12. Halberstam, "Wild Beyond," 8.

witnessing to "the other thing, the other world, the joyful noise of the scattered, scattered eschaton" to which he belonged and helped create.[13]

What Baltrop ultimately witnessed in his photography was an "idiosyncratic, aesthetically sophisticated, and historically significant body of work that is sui generis: a dual portrait of a man's life and of a New York City that no longer exists."[14] Said differently, Baltrop's body is in his body of work, and his body cannot be so easily separated from the bodies in his work. As Wilcox notes, what Baltrop produced was a "diaristic and deeply personal body of work."[15]

When Baltrop first discovered the world in the piers, he confessed that he was terrified. But after his fear passed, Baltrop was seized by a determination "to preserve the frightening, mad, unbelievable, violent, and beautiful things that were going on at that time."[16] His terror and deep feeling suggested that he was not some disinterested bystander, but one who recognized something of who he was in the world.

The Undercommons of the piers beckoned to him, and Baltrop answered. Quitting his day job as a taxi driver and living out of his van so that he could live there for days at a time, he developed sophisticated techniques to capture the world that unfolded around him. Moreover, Baltrop gave all of himself to capturing this world. Art critic and curator Valerie Cassel Oliver notes that "for over a decade, [Baltrop] committed himself to photographing the complex of dilapidated buildings that extended from Tribeca to West 59th Street. The intensity of Baltrop's engagement was staggering, bordering upon the obsessive."[17] Baltrop often "hung from the ceilings of several warehouses utilizing a makeshift harness, watching and waiting for hours to record the lives that these people led."[18] It was crucial for Baltrop to be able to record those as he saw them, as he recognized himself in them, and his photographs invite us to do the same, to see ourselves in the bodies he lovingly documents, as bodies "in motion, in between various modes of being and belonging."[19] Thus as Crimp

13. Halberstam, "Wild Beyond," 10.
14. Wilcox, afterword, 57.
15. Wilcox, afterword, 57.
16. Douglas Crimp, "Douglas Crimp on Alvin Baltrop," *Artforum*, February 1, 2008, https://www.mutualart.com/Article/DOUGLAS-CRIMP-ON-ALVIN-BALTROP/3FDF CA24DD6FDC1F.
17. Cassel Oliver, "Alvin Baltrop," 14. Hereafter, references to this source will appear in the text.
18. Crimp, "Douglas Crimp on Alvin Baltrop."
19. Halberstam, "Wild Beyond," 5.

states, "you don't *feel* that Baltrop's project was documentary in nature";[20] Baltrop was most definitely not one of the "outsiders and the uplifters" who "fail to capture it, to get it right" (Hartman). Baltrop created the world in which he "himself [is] a denizen of the piers, immersed in the scene."[21]

From within and immersed in the world, Baltrop revealed those around him, those labeled social deviants and rejects as sacred subjects through his practice of attentive looking. Baltrop was deeply patient and loving in his photographic gaze, imbuing the marginalized and the maligned with grace and dignity through careful use of light and shadows. Baltrop was deeply familiar with the residents and visitors of the piers, and he created their "portraits with such authenticity and empathy that their gazes are wide open, neither defiant nor shielded. They see in Baltrop what he sees in them. There is no judgment, no resistance, nor a need to justify their existence" (Cassel Oliver, 14). Baltrop's loving gaze is a practice that makes sacred, that makes the beloved, which recalls the words of poet Gregory Orr:

> When the world
> For a single moment
> Focuses on you,
> You become the beloved.[22]

The untitled photograph of three nude males is a great example of Baltrop's patience and willingness to wait for hours at a time to capture the perfect moment.[23] A young man glows as he is lying on his stomach with legs splayed so far apart that his scrotum is visible. Even so, he is resplendent in his vulnerability. His private parts are both exposed and covered by light. Light falls on the other two bodies as well, though not as lavishly. The light on the teenage boy's body in the middle highlights his form; he seems taut and tense. He hugs his elbows and appears vulnerable. I would like to see his face but I can only see his profile. He remains unreadable despite his nakedness. The man on the right seems poised for action. He appears much older and stronger and cuts an imposing figure because he is the only one standing. Unlike the other two who are barefoot, he is wearing socks and shoes, or at least he is

20. Crimp, preface to *Alvin Baltrop*, 11, emphasis mine.

21. Crimp, preface to *Alvin Baltrop*, 11.

22. Gregory Orr, "Concerning the Book That Is the Body of the Beloved: Document View," *The Virginia Quarterly Review* 81, no. 2 (2005): 4.

23. This photograph can be viewed at http://nealbaercollection.org/the-piers-three-men -on-a-dock/.

The Piers (two men sitting) *(c. 1975–86) by Alvin Baltrop, © 2023 Estate of Alvin Baltrop /*
Artists Rights Society (ARS), New York

on his left foot, suggesting that he is not fully at home in the space. The three
bodies are composed in such a way that adheres to the "rule of three," but the
middle body is positioned off-center to disrupt harmony. The tension of the
scene is enhanced because the faces of the figures are turned away, not just
from each other but also from the viewer. Baltrop suffuses the three figures
with mystery and elusiveness even as they are resplendently naked before our
eyes. He reminds us that they cannot be fully known, that they are more than
what we see or imagine.

In another photograph, the viewer is invited to espy a scene of forbidden
love between two men.[24] A voyeuristic feel is achieved by the soft focus and
distance, suggesting the usage of a zoom lens. The viewer peeks into an interracial couple whose naked bodies are enmeshed in a scene of sexual intimacy.
Here, also, the use of light makes the lovers glow amid a shadowy world of
decay. The dark pools on the floor and the shadows of dark steel structure add
to the mood of doom and disintegration. The couple occupies just a sliver of
compositional space and thus appears both vulnerable and engulfed by the vast
entanglement of steel structure above and the wooden boards streaked with
shadows. Their embrace defies the cold barrenness of their surroundings. The

24. This photograph can be viewed at https://images.app.goo.gl/wx1tpm3ibyAH9PKh9.

look of tenderness and delight on the face of the Black man as he leans over the White man witnesses to a "sporadic joy" that could be found in human touch amid decay and darkness.

My favorite picture of Baltrop's is the one of two figures sitting closely on a platform, their backs against the viewer. They appear achingly small even as they appear to glimmer in the vast space of the darkness. Their bodies bespeak resignation, tiredness. I can make out the hands of the right figure resting on his or her knees while the one on the left slouches forward. They seem so small, fragile, and forgotten. But I sense a deep communion even in the midst of such desolation. I like to imagine that they are holding each other's hands and resting in that small sense of belonging.

Baltrop refused to give up on the piers because of the belonging he found there, because Baltrop knew that the world of the piers was "extraordinary" (Cassel Oliver, 14). He shot "thousands of images of the piers—interiors and exteriors, the exuberance of sexual encounters and the unexpected tragedies" (14). And he recorded and captured the piers, motivated by nothing but love. Baltrop was poor all his life; he would make nothing from his photographs, and whatever Baltrop had, he spent in developing prints, conjuring visions of this alternative community. Baltrop was part of organizing groups that sought to save the piers when it was under the threat of being torn down. And when the piers were eventually razed in 1985, Baltrop turned to preserve the memories of this world through continuing to print his photographs as well as "collecting oral histories from those living or cruising along the piers" (15).

It is a tragedy that Baltrop was able to print just a small sample of the tens of thousands of photos he captured in the decade he haunted the piers. But what he could afford to print, Baltrop did so carefully, "until he achieved the texture and emotional tenor he sought" (14). Wilcox recalls that Baltrop was often overcome by pain when looking at his own work because he was reminded of the stories of the people. "There are *so* many stories," Baltrop said. Wilcox shares that "Baltrop exposed himself to his subjects as much as they exposed themselves to him. In fact, friends and neighbors noted, he was one of them." He had more than just their consent when it came to the photographs; he was beloved and "remembered to have known the story of everyone he photographed." In fact, there were even some who "took off their clothes and demanded to be photographed."[25]

I am haunted by those who asked to be photographed, those who said to Baltrop, "Take a picture of me." I wonder if they trembled as they fumbled

25. Wilcox in Atoe, "Alvin Baltrop."

out of their clothes, allowing everything to fall to the ground except for their nakedness. I imagine someone saying, "This is my body." I imagine the communion of being seen and seeing to be as thrilling and forgiving as joining a band of naked children washing each other as they dance under the abundance of rainfall.

Works Cited

Atoe, Osa. "Alvin Baltrop: A Queer Black Photographer's Groundbreaking Work Comes to Life Five Years after His Death." *Colorlines*, March 24, 2009. https://www.colorlines.com/articles/alvin-baltrop.

Baltrop, Alvin. *Alvin Baltrop: Dreams into Glass*. Edited by Valerie Cassel Oliver. Perspectives 179. Houston: Contemorary Arts Museum, 2012.

Cassel Oliver, Valerie. "Alvin Baltrop: Dreams into Glass." In Baltrop, *Alvin Baltrop: Dreams into Glass*, 13–15.

Crimp, Douglas. "Douglas Crimp on Alvin Baltrop." *Artforum,* February 1, 2008. https://www.mutualart.com/Article/DOUGLAS-CRIMP-ON-ALVIN-BAL TROP/3FDFCA24DD6FDC1F.

———. Preface to *Alvin Baltrop: Dreams into Glass*, by Alvin Baltrop, 11.

Halberstam, Jack. "The Wild Beyond: With and for the Undercommons." In *The Undercommons: Fugitive Planning & Black Study,* by Stefano Harney and Fred Moten, 7–12. New York: Minor Composition, 2013.

Hartman, Saidiya. "The Terrible Beauty of the Slum." *Brick: A Literary Journal*, July 28, 2017. https://brickmag.com/the-terrible-beauty-of-the-slum/.

Orr, Gregory. "Concerning the Book That Is the Body of the Beloved: Document View." *The Virginia Quarterly Review* 81, no. 2 (2005): 4.

Swanson, Carl. "Manhattan's West Side Piers, Back When They Were Naked and Gay." *New York Magazine*, November 18, 2015. http://nymag.com/daily/intel ligencer/2015/11/west-side-piers-when-they-were-naked-and-gay.html.

Wilcox, Randal. Afterword. In Baltrop, *Alvin Baltrop: Dreams into Glass*, 57–58.

10

God-Talk and Lorde-Speak

Audre Lorde and Inappropriate Theopoetics

OLUWATOMISIN OLAYINKA OREDEIN

As a theologian I have noticed a pattern of practice in Christian theological,[1] ethical, and biblical interpretive scholars' attempts to be interdisciplinary: impactful voices, and subsequently their ideas, are brought into conversation with persons and subjects they are not directly addressing or engaging. While this practice is frankly commonplace, it is also curious in that, many times, these voices are made interlocutors in conversations I do not believe would be of interest to them. I am not sure they would spend their time or use their ideas in these respective debates. I say this precisely because within their work, *they* do not say this; those of us engaging them bring them into the room and make them the head of the table, a table they may not have approached if not conceptually situated there.

One person I have noticed this pattern with is the inimitable Audre Lorde. Because she is truth-telling and truth-seeking, and she wisely speaks to areas beyond her direct textual engagement, she is alluring to many disciplinary voices—especially theologians talking about Blackness or Black life, especially theologians interested in engaging theology liberatively, differently, creatively. This Caribbean American poet whose work signals contact with Christianity in various points resonates fascinatingly well with those of us interested in

1. When speaking of "theology," I am referring to Christian theology in the US context.

the field of theopoetics, an area of theological discourse that argues toward theological meaning-making in its daring to—through innovative moves and pursuits—create new or underexplored waves of God-talk.

It seems that I am making a big deal out of nothing: interlocutive scholarship is the norm, today, is even a sign of rigorous engagement. This may be true, but interlocutive scholarship not only pinpoints whose voice is valued enough to dialogue with but also determines the why behind the value placed on the interlocutor's own viewpoint. As scholars, especially those of us in theopoetics, what we leave out or forget in order to forge the narrative we think worth knowing is critical to pause and sit with. Oftentimes, what is missing in scholarship that does not consider the trajectory of another's voice, and thus their respective interest, is a humanizing regard. Would this person "be here" if we did not bring them "here"? What does the pattern of their scholarship show us about where *they* would want to be? We scholars engage ideas born from lives with particular experiences. This is the case with Lorde; her ideological directions were quite intentional. What I wonder is, Why are we not always aware that this directional intentionality is *also* the case with the theopoetic scholar?

If one moves too quickly to use Lorde and does not offer a deep enough reflection of oneself *in using her voice*, the task of theopoetics grows small. What is being made but replicas of colonial theology uninterested or unable to ask the question, What am I seeing in *needing* to see and use what Lorde is seeing?

We Need

So, I ask again: Why do *we* in the field of Christian theology and its subfields, such as theopoetics, *need* Audre Lorde?

She never called herself a theopoet. In some ways, those of us in Christian theology *need* to call her that, or at least associate her with the discipline, for she adds something to the prophetic potential of liberative theological outlooks. She did not purposefully enter into this conversation about how Black women's wisdom can enhance contributions in Christian theology and its branches; the gaps in the discourse brought her in.

What is Christian theology doing *in* this?

It is following the path to free up God-talk. Christian theology needs to be liberated, so we theologians revere the woman whose language sounds so close to liberation's potential, whose expression echoing the theological seems unbound by theology's ideational parameters.

But to blame theological discourse, as the main pull, alone would be dishonest—I think it is us. *We* brought her here. We theologians need her to do something *for us*. We sacralize what she represents that we cannot quite access within our respective discipline and on our own accord—words and body unfettered by religious boundaries—a living word.

It seems that Lorde's voice gives us theologians permission to theologize in a different direction, one attentive to corporal details.

It seems that she grants us creative hermeneutical permission; thus we take Lorde's words and ideas to infuse our own theologically compressed ideas and words with sound and worth, depth and volume.

And we do this because the primary point of contact we *may* share with her is critical to the heart of Christian theologizing: flesh.

We put her at the table, and in this forceful invitation, we invoke Lorde's flesh,[2] that dynamic entity conceptually wider than the body alone, theologian Myra Rivera suggests.[3]

We aim to invoke flesh as that which is good and has holy potential, or that has theological possibility at the very least[4]—flesh not bound by dialogical stasis. Flesh that is dynamic and not unmoved.

But this flesh business is risky. Though theologians and ethicists see dialogical potential, the risk of Lorde's being *invoked* in this way instead of invited can begin treading a dangerous path.

In my conversation pieces for this chapter, "Poetry Is Not a Luxury" and "Uses of the Erotic," Lorde speaks of herself and other Black women in terms of a "self." Some may translate or hear something closer to the term "body." I want to think of it in terms of "flesh."

---

2. I am thinking flesh here as a nod to the erotic as well as on an ontological dimension. Lorde is clear in her writing that she brings all of herself, including that which constitutes her self—her shyness, her strength, her fatness, her generosity, her loyalty, her crotchetiness—as a means of bringing all of who she is into her writing in order to grant that writing essential worth. The experience of herself, including the details of her fleshliness, adds value to her words. See Audre Lorde, "Poetry Makes Something Happen," in *I Am Your Sister: Collected and Unpublished Writings of Audre Lorde*, ed. Rudolph P. Byrd, Johnnetta Betsch Cole, and Beverly Guy-Sheftall (Oxford: Oxford University Press, 2011), 184.

3. In my two primary essays/pieces of focus, "Poetry Is Not a Luxury" and "Uses of the Erotic: The Erotic as Power," from *Sister Outsider: Essays and Speeches* (Berkeley: Crossing, 2007), Lorde does not utilize language of "the body," but of "self/selves." I think the way she is describing the self aligns closely with Rivera's notion of "flesh," hence my experimenting with applying this language to Lorde's ideas.

4. Mayra Rivera, "Introduction: Both Flesh and Not," in *Poetics of the Flesh* (Durham, NC: Duke University Press, 2015), 1–2.

For Lorde, flesh is not a matter of Christian conversation, but ontology *recognized* as divine in itself. In talking with her and interacting with her work, I do not think we understand what we are getting into, but we are so keen on invoking that which many of us are still striving toward, but may never know: flesh unbound.

I wonder if Lorde would care about our theological wonderings, or if in her work, she is simply trying to affirm *her* flesh.

I wonder if we are *allowed* to use her affirmation and conclusions toward ulterior affirmations and conclusions, ones that ironically may tighten their grip on that from which Lorde is trying to break free: category, boundaries—in Christian theology's case, the unwavering locus of divinity.

To use Black women's flesh in order to flesh out the sacralizing work of another's flesh can create flesh dominance. Though Lorde's interests seem to be on the fundamental path to simply love *her* flesh, she is used to bolster the message of a discipline dominated by voices who may not even recognize her flesh as good.

I say this because Lorde's work *is* fleshy, literally and conceptually. Women like Lorde, Black women, who expose the vulnerabilities of their lives in their work, risk themselves and their voices being taken and used for another's sanctifying mission. This is often the case with minoritized persons: their work is not merely *work*; it is their life. It is their body—their story, their essence. Lorde reminds us, "I write my living and I live my work."[5]

For some of us who do not know the trauma of a body like Lorde's, we take and eat (of her) in hopes that in this ritualistic capturing, *we* can be transformed.

There is theo-logic behind why we need Lorde: we need her flesh to interpret our theological frames anew. But I wonder if there is also more, if there is theology to be found and transformed *in itself* in understanding not only how Lorde's message and process can (further) liberate theology, but also in recognizing how theologizing is a totalizing, corporeal reality.

Theology cannot function on *parts* of our existence. It needs all of the flesh, in its dynamism and even chaos, in order to transform; it needs the fullness of one's being in order to be understood on a soul level[6] or at least to not summon the rigidity of death.[7]

---

5. Audre Lorde, "Poetry Makes Something Happen," in Byrd, Betsch Cole, and Guy-Sheftall, *I Am Your Sister*, 184.

6. Lorde, "Poetry Makes Something Happen," 184.

7. Audre Lorde, "Self-Definition and My Poetry," in Byrd, Betsch Cole, and Guy-Sheftall, *I Am Your Sister*, 157.

In our engaging Lorde I am assuming we are not confident that Western Christian theology as we know it can give this to us.

A THEOPOETIC WORD

What I call "inappropriate theopoetics" then is perhaps the closest conversation we can have to what, I believe, Lorde does in her writing.

This is how I know theopoetics.

Theopoetics is the creative activity of God-talk. It is a reminder that divine lessons can be found wherever the assumption of God's location and movement are no longer regimented or bound. It is an invitation for that which has traditionally been sectioned off to the margins of serious theological inquiry, an embodied theological process, to help name the truth about God's reach and manifestation.

Theopoetics is multiform, has multiple identities and in this, limitlessness (for each identity has a breadth of revelation within itself). It is a means of showing that one has permission to use *all* of their imagination, *all* of their life circumstances and events, *all* of their identity, *all* of their questions and wonderings to find their way to and to talk about God.

Its variation is in its means, its process, its form. These routes are theological as much as the insight they may yield.

The creative means, the liberated process, the distinct form that theopoetics may take hold theological elements themselves, illuminating the journey and the vehicle as just as relevant as, if not more important than, the final destination.

Thus, theopoetics is theology done in freedom of process, without a uniform guide of formal method. To be clear, for some voices in theopoetics, its expression *may* follow a more formal method, but for others, the creative means and action through which God-truth is revealed *is* the point.

Theopoetics is theology allowed to wander around—on tongues, in bodies, and in art. The unboundedness of theopoetics, its refusal to fit categorically into one identifiable mode of doing theology, renders it confusing in some traditional theological circles, inappropriate in many.

FROM A. LORDE

This is not why Lorde is an inappropriate theopoet, however. Her sensations are inappropriate.

In "Poetry Is Not a Luxury" and "Uses of the Erotic," she follows feeling religiously, and in this, honors the guidance of her flesh toward the divine that looks Black, loves lesbian—the divine so close to her body, it reverberates through her flesh, sourced as not external to her, but intimately within.

This sourcing *does not work* with Christian theology traditionally considered. For many of us, *feeling* theology through points of ontological tension is typically not a thing, but for Lorde, it is the *main* thing. *Her flesh* is it—the site of questioning and the place of liberating revelation.

"As a Black, lesbian, feminist, socialist, poet, mother of two, including one boy, and a member of an interracial couple," Lorde writes, "I usually find myself part of some group in which the majority defines me as deviant, difficult, inferior, or just plain 'wrong.'"[8] The same can be said for her voice's fit within Christian theological canon; she has too many parts to herself. This volume of detail does not fit, is inappropriate.

Given the complex contours of her identity, belonging is not a viable option for Lorde's ontological imagination, but self-definition is. Because of how her particular flesh fits no social form, she self-determines the shape of her freedom. The sense of empowerment that the circumstances of her life have issued her, is hers to own.[9]

This can translate into divine proclamation of the sort to which Christianity is not typically accustomed. Lorde does not need the Western conception of God or the formal structures of theology to understand the sacredness of the world in and around her. *She is* the source through which she understands the holiness of the world. Every aspect of her flesh, her experience, and her life gift her with a sacred lens.

Her flesh holds lifeforce, "creative energy empowered."[10] She can create new life with her words. This idea, similar in feeling to a Genesis 1 moment, implements the freedom for life to emerge from "extrapolations and recognitions from within ourselves."[11] Her words, born from "a dark place within, where hidden and growing [our] true spirit rises"[12]—hovers over the face of the deep well of Christian assumptions of divine source and says otherwise.

---

8. Audre Lorde, "There Is No Hierarchy of Oppression," in Byrd, Betsch Cole, and Guy-Sheftall, *I Am Your Sister*, 219–20.

9. Audre Lorde, "Commencement Address: Oberlin College, May 29, 1989," in Byrd, Betsch Cole, and Guy-Sheftall, *I Am Your Sister*, 218.

10. Lorde, "Uses of the Erotic," 55.

11. Lorde, "Poetry Is Not a Luxury," 38.

12. Lorde, "Poetry Is Not a Luxury," 36.

We, her readers, can feel it. She does not need Christian theology—at least traditionally considered and conceptualized. It is *we who need her* to tell us that how we encounter the divine does not require the fences we have put around its conceptualization.

We see the tricky dance of an ulterior, other-sourced theology, her self-divinity a reinforcement of *her* selfhood. Remember, Lorde never called herself a theopoet. We do, for we see characteristics of Christianity both within her and yet outside of how *she* theologizes.

Her divine subject is herself. There is no religious claim she tries to make, but it is the claim of us, those with theological background, as the divine in her explication of herself is too omnipresent to ignore, her erotic power too boundless to be bound. This has nothing to do with Lorde and everything to do with us. We cannot help but see a divine message in the power of her desire for autonomy and authenticity.

She wrests Christian theology's power, as *we* have brought it into the conversation, from *its* hands in her holding the power over the message of *her* life. She emanates divinity, because given the holiness of her liberation in her flesh, she recognizes her divine potential.[13]

Her liberated tongue and how she lovingly knows her flesh echo Christian aspiration. Again, this is why she is so appealing.

TO BE FREE

Lorde's empowerment is seen and felt through her living unapologetically and fully embodied; this comes through powerfully in her writing. The divine-shadowing is not only in her description of herself, but in its generative power.

Lorde creates as she writes, her poetry a "revelatory distillation of experience"[14] that, as she remarks, "makes you happen."[15] This creative movement comes from what she knows—through understanding her flesh and all therein, as the good journey, the vehicle to which she arrives at her destination: liberation.

The theopoetic connection might be made *here*. We can leave her revelations alone (and not try to make them something else) but watch what she does, and in this *learn how to love the flesh of our theologies*.

13. Lorde, "Uses of the Erotic," 54.
14. Lorde, "Poetry Is Not a Luxury," 37.
15. Lorde, "Poetry Makes Something Happen," 184.

Writing from the space of her flesh, from the core of the erotic—this is the greatest lesson Lorde teaches us about the theological capability and parameters under which many of us are so used to operating. The flesh's untapped power is the precise avenue through which divine knowing is possible. For Lorde the flesh tells divine stories of itself if we are willing to love her, honor her, liberate her to herself.

Lorde does not apologize for her flesh; she celebrates it. She does not invite others to determine what it should be; she shares with the world all of who *she* is and calls it empowered, chaotic, exceeding the self, and the best route to living.

Lorde is inappropriate because *she does not need* Christian theology's ultimate parameters or permission to exist as she wants and as she has chosen: she needs no trinitarian validation about the truth of her life. Her flesh, her Black female flesh, her Black female lesbian flesh is revelatory enough. The dynamism and movement of the flesh as she lives into it is not a problem, but a sharpened lens. If "the erotic is the measure between the beginnings of our sense of self and the chaos of our strongest feelings," Lorde is content to flow in between self and sensation. Affective liminality is not to be feared but drawn upon as a resource of empowerment. It does not need male energy or affirmation behind it, in discourse or otherwise.

Lorde shows Christian theologians and theopoets how to write from flesh that is torn, for something akin to healing *will* emanate forth—not Christian theology per se, but a mode and model from which to understand that that which we feel *is* theologizing.

Speak the truth from the flesh, the feminine flesh. From here we can understand that words offered up are not vehicles transporting customary notions, but serious voyagers carrying sacredness in their fabric.

The liberation of being uncategorical: this is the promise from which Christian theology can learn. The audacity to fully be, declare such iterations of existence holy and worthy of good words and outright praise. This *feels* theological. This invites the process of divine recognition in the ordinary and in places that theological treatise or trains of thought have absentmindedly bypassed.

Speaking truth to power is speaking in the tongue of flesh.

Alas, this is inappropriate theopoetics: accepting the invitation to a fleshy journey, content to travel beyond and leave behind what the rest of the world, the rest of society, deems suitable shores.

Works Cited

Byrd, Rudolph P., Johnnetta Betsch Cole, and Beverly Guy-Sheftall, eds. *I Am Your Sister: Collected and Unpublished Writings of Audre Lorde*. Oxford: Oxford University Press, 2011.

Lorde, Audre. "Commencement Address: Oberlin College, May 29, 1989." In Byrd, Betsch Cole, and Guy-Sheftall, *I Am Your Sister*, 213–18.

———. "Poetry Is Not a Luxury." In Lorde, *Sister Outsider*, 32–35.

———. "Poetry Makes Something Happen." In Byrd, Betsch Cole, and Guy-Sheftall, *I Am Your Sister*, 184–87.

———. "Self-Definition and My Poetry." In Byrd, Betsch Cole, and Guy-Sheftall, *I Am Your Sister*, 156–57.

———. *Sister Outsider: Essays and Speeches*. Berkeley: Crossing, 1984.

———. "There Is No Hierarchy of Oppression." In Byrd, Betsch Cole, and Guy-Sheftall, *I Am Your Sister*, 219–20.

———. "Uses of the Erotic: The Erotic as Power." In Lorde, *Sister Outsider*, 49–55.

Rivera, Mayra. *Poetics of the Flesh*. Durham, NC: Duke University Press, 2015.

Part 4

HERMENEUTICS, PROCLAMATION, AND CLAIM

11

Potluck Theology

A Theopoetic of Fullness

JOYCE DEL ROSARIO

My embodied epistemology was developed under the care and tutelage of the sixty or so members of my Filipino American extended family. As I look back, the most spiritually formative practice I can remember and still enjoy today is our family potluck.

CALL TO WORSHIP

Our homes are sacred. "Take off your sandals, for the place where you are standing is holy ground" (Exod. 3:5 NIV). As young children we learned how to take our shoes off upon entering someone's house. Practically, it is a way to show respect to the homeowner by helping keep the floors clean. Culturally, it is a tradition practiced by many Asian homes around the world. As I got older, I realized it is also a ritual sign that we are leaving our lives outside and entering into a new presence with one another. Taking off our shoes is a way for us to leave our White-dominant American world behind as we prepare to join one another.

As I take off my own shoes, I also balance a hot dish of my potluck offering. I see the shoe pile of those who have entered before me, reminding me that I no longer need to assimilate here; I am with kin. We enter the house and have permission to become our whole selves in the safety of a family member's home. We can speak Tagalog or English or Taglish if we like, we could eat what we like, and we could joke around how we like. We do not need to explain ourselves or make ourselves smaller here. The sacred space of our Filipino family home is a place where we do not have to look less Brown or speak with a "better English accent." At home, at our homes, we are enough.

Taking off our shoes signaled to ourselves and to others that we were now present in someone's home, someone's sacred space, the place where Godself dwells among us, the Holy of Holies. This was not our office or classroom or gym; it was a family member's home. The home for which they worked night shifts at the hospital or post office. Our homes are the manifestation of the American dream. The home where they are not the minority or someone who cannot speak English (we can), but a place where *we* are the dominant culture and our languages are spoken here and our foods are eaten here. In our socks and bare feet, we connect to the holy ground of our homes.

Passing the Peace, Passing Our Piece

In church, when we shake hands, "passing the peace" feels a little more Western and frankly a bit physically removed. We turn around in the pews and shake the hands of visitors and members alike. "Peace be with you," we say. It is cordial, but a little aloof. As an introvert, I find this part of the church service also mildly terrifying.

However, I notice that there is a distinct change in my way of responding to someone when I give them a kiss on the cheek or a hug. The kiss on the cheek is so intimate to me because it is how I greet my parents, my aunties and uncles, and the elders at our potlucks. We were taught to greet each other this way as a sign of respect, as a sign of love. The tenderness of a kiss on the cheek is disarming even to the strictest of relatives.

When I greet others with a handshake it feels distant and formal. It is almost offensive to pass the peace with such a distant gesture. What kind of peace am I giving as I stand a foot away from the person? I have room to defend myself and stay guarded with a handshake. I am vulnerable and susceptible to you if I kiss you on the cheek.

A kiss on the cheek is a disarming act. It is an act of love. It is an act of sharing ourselves, accompanied by an embrace. It is the moment where I let my guard down and share a piece of myself. It is a ritual of what we call *kapwa,* or our sense of belonging to one another. Our belonging is much like the African idea of *ubuntu,* "I am because we are." Our existence is bound up in one another. Our existence is informed by one another. The kiss on the cheek as we come and go from each other's presence is not just a passing of peace, but a passing of a piece of ourselves.

This passing of our "piece" starts at a young age. We were taught from a young age to enter the room and kiss each family member as a greeting. It can take a few minutes as we make our way around the room to greet each and every relative we may (or may not) know. The ritual is again repeated at the end as we leave the home, kissing each person goodbye, or "make *paalam*" as the aunties say. That is, we give notice that we are leaving the presence of the family.

In more traditional families and for older family members, we would also *mano* them. This is the ritual of taking the elder's (or highly respected person's, such as a priest's) hand and taking the back of their hand to one's forehead in an act of asking for their blessing. Asking for blessing and kissing on the cheek are ways of passing our piece and asking for peace. We share our love. We share our blessings. We share pieces of ourselves with one another.

Words with God

As we gather around the potluck table, we situate ourselves so we can see each person's face as we stand in a large circle holding hands. There is a quick scan of the room to see who should give the prayer before the meal. The first honor goes to the pastor. The next priority of order is the matriarch—the eldest woman, usually a *Lola* (grandmother) of the group. In the absence of a pastor (male or female), the women are seen as the spiritual leaders. Traditionally, they are the heads of the household when it comes to finances and caretaking, so the spiritual head becomes a natural role to take as well.

In our family potlucks, the prayer before the meal is like the sermon in a service. The honor of simultaneously speaking to God on behalf of the group and speaking to the group on behalf of God goes to the spiritual leader present. The leadership learned at our family gatherings was that it was the women who were in charge.

At our roots, Filipinos are an egalitarian culture. Any patriarchy in our communities has come from Catholic church systems, but as a culture we tend to be more egalitarian if not truly a matriarchy, at least within the household and extended family systems. United Methodists have long ordained women, and although I did not have a female pastor until my adult years, I never felt the limitations that would discourage me from answering the call to ordination should that ever happen.

Joyce del Rosario

Communion

Following the words with God is the communion. All are welcome to the table.

I learned what the word "communion" meant when we gathered as a family around the potluck table. The whole act of being together was communion in and of itself. And when the food was ready and the families were present, we gathered around the table.

As in Catholic traditions of Mass where the Eucharist is the highest part of the liturgy, so too is our gathering around the table with one another. Communion. Co-union with me.

It is in this interaction of balancing my plate, while walking around the table, scooping small samples of dish after dish. The first thing I put on is the rice; always steamed white rice. We have at least two ten-cup rice cookers at the ready. I am careful not to get too much so I have room on my plate for the next fifteen dishes on the table. The next item might be salad. Maybe the strawberry vinaigrette salad that Auntie Cecil makes. Or maybe some form of ambrosia salad, full of canned fruits and whipped cream and a nod to the American colonization of the Philippines.

I often bring baked salmon. Uncle Dan brings the prime rib or the turkey, depending on the occasion. Auntie Cecil brings her *lumpia*, "fresh" *lumpia*, meaning not fried and full of vegetables. For Christmas, Lori brings her cathedral gelatin, layers of gelatin shaped like Christmas trees. Each thin layer stacked on top of each other; red then white then green then white again and then another red and white layer. All stacked like a beautiful terrine. This is a version derived from the traditional cathedral cakes; white gelatin Bundt cakes. With sparkling green and red cubes floating in the midst of the white gelatin, mimicking the stained-glass windows of the cathedral churches in the Philippines.

Then of course there would be fried *lumpia*, crispy and as golden brown as our skin. Someone, probably an uncle, would be posted outside, with their hand on one hip, frying *lumpia* to keep the whole house from smelling even though the smell of pork and the crackling sounds of oil can make one's mouth water. However, we did not want the smell to linger for another week after. Frying vinegar-marinated milkfish also has a way of lingering long past our gatherings. I had a non-Filipino friend once comment that our house often smelled like rice and garlic. That is truly the smell of home to me. Maybe that is the smell of immigrant homes in general. It is the smell of an invitation to stay and eat. The smells of garlic, onions, bay leaves, peppers, and spices embedded into the walls and carpets are the constant invitation to co-union. It is the smell of a nourished home.

We co-union as a family, as *Lolos* and *Lolas*, *Titas* (aunts) and *Titos* (uncles), *magpinsan* (cousins), *magkapitid* (brothers and sisters), and *mga apo* (grandchildren). The smells and tastes of the sour and sweet and unctuous comingle as we eat. It all matters. We all matter. Because without rice, the adobo does not taste the same. Without the salty tang of mangoes and tomatoes, the pork would be too rich. In a potluck, we need each other's dishes. In life, we need one another. Our belonging to each other is what makes sense. It is how I see God. In fact this is how I understand abundance. We always have more than we need. The tradition of sending people back with the leftovers or *baon*. That is the idea of sending people home with a blessing. Sending people home with more than what was needed. The leftover baskets of bread and fish like Jesus served to the five thousand.

This is the blessing. This is where we are filled—filled with the spirit, filled with the body of Christ, filled with the blood of Christ, filled with our time together. It is in our eating with one another that we celebrate one another. We celebrate who the other person is. We celebrate our families. We celebrate the ability to even gather together at all. We celebrate having made it through another year. We celebrate new babies. We celebrate new marriages. We celebrate the life of people who have passed away before. It is here that we truly commune with each other. We co-union with each other. We are not individuals coming together; we are one.

Communion of Saints

Our *kapwa* is our sense of belonging to one another. It is our sense of being because of the other. The African sense of *ubuntu* may be more widely known as a way of existing in the collective for the collective. For Filipino/a/xs our *kapwa* extends to our ancestors. We are who we are because of those who have gone before us. The sacrifices they made to set up the next generation for a better life do not go unnoticed. *Lola's* sternness to one cousin and abundant love for another cousin has a way of shaping our self-understanding.

I remember *Lola* Ruth and *Lola* Alice sitting at the table at our family gatherings. They were sisters who had raised their families in the Philippines and were now living with those extended families in the United States. They said little at the parties, but they were thinking a lot. They smiled when I greeted them with a kiss on the cheek. Today, long after they have passed on, they remain with us, watching us, sharing food with us, listening to their great grandchildren run around.

My dad is among those saints now. A few short days after he passed away, we were in my mother's living room. Many of us had gathered to eat dinner and keep my mom company in the time of grief. My cousins and I were sitting on the couch near the front door. At one point, the door handle distinctly turned and the door moved open. My cousins and I looked at each other in surprise. It was not the wind, because the door handle turned. We all saw that happen. I took a deep breath, and welcomed my father into his home. It was as if he did not want to miss the party either. Our *kapwa* is so strong, death could not separate us from being in the presence of one another.

CREED

As children we were taught a type of creed that grounds us and our connection with one another.

> I believe that children are a major part of the life of the church. I believe that children are the LIFE of the church. I believe that we respect our elders and give them due honor. I believe in sharing what we have with one another in a spirit of generosity.
>
> I believe regularly gathering together is important to the body of Christ.
>
> I believe soul food allows us to share pieces of our souls with one another through our serving and consuming of each dish.
>
> I believe in bringing our best to the table and not what is easiest so we can all share in the goodness of one another.
>
> I believe in the transformational power of co-unioning over a good meal.
>
> I believe that the presence of God is found in the presence of one another.
>
> I believe that there is more than one main dish.
>
> I believe that side dishes are not subaltern to main dishes, but make the other dishes better.
>
> I believe that my family gatherings are what the Holy of Holies feels like.

BENEDICTION

May the Lord feast with you, and you with one another, now and forevermore. Amen.

12

"Mi Abuela Decía . . ."

Inheriting Life and Faith through Popular Refrains

YARA GONZÁLEZ-JUSTINIANO

The use of refrains and popular sayings is not exclusive to Latin American cultures. However, within some of these cultures, I argue, certain refrains shed light on both particular and important spiritual practices of transcendence and function as containers of tradition and knowledge. They serve as sources of wisdom, tradition, and cultural resistance that unearth a theopoetics—a way of talking about the divine—that breaks religious structures and connects to a spirituality that transcends and weaves Latinx people as a group.[1] These refrains and popular sayings, often neatly packaged one-liners, contain worlds of knowledge that allow faith, values, and ethics to be traditioned and shared— sometimes unnoticed—while being retained in memory amid cultural imperialism in the United States and other contexts with similar sociopolitical dynamics. In this chapter, I will elaborate on some of these refrains and how they contain theological truths and existential wisdom for Latin American communities, in particular, Spanish refrains in Puerto Rican culture. This chapter is divided into two main categories. First is function, which briefly lays out what refrains do in culture and how they operate. And second is grounding, elaborating what the refrain's content is saying and traditioning in its cultural body.

---

1. My focus on sayings in Spanish is a case study. This does not represent all generations or ethnicities of Latinx in the United States due to the diversity that exists in this group.

Refrains give a sense of community that is not about pointing to its origins but about carrying meaning and function in society. In the work of paremiology (the study of proverbs), history, and ideology of refrains, Puerto Rican writer Wenceslao Serra Deliz summarizes how different cultures use popular refrains and sayings.[2] He argues that the real purpose of refrains is found in their use and gives examples across cultures and countries. In Nigerian Yoruba tribes, for example, people use their refrains as a rite of passage into adulthood signaling a transition of both societal and spiritual terrains.[3] Similarly in Puerto Rico, though not signified with the same ritualistic practices, speaking in refrains can be seen as a sign of adulthood, since most adults and elders speak in refrains and riddles. Whenever my mother is about to impart some wisdom she begins with the qualifier, "mi abuela decía" (my grandmother used to say). There is—in theory—no rigidity of use, meaning, or even a single author; however, these refrains also rely on a form of authority, be it the messenger or the message itself. Serra Deliz also argues that, in Panamá, the generalized use of refrains affirms their use across social classes.[4] By this, it does not mean that refrains are generally applicable to all classes equally but that those that remain as a form of cultural identity do not belong nor are used by solely one socioeconomic class; for example, the expression "¡Ay Bendito!" in Puerto Rico, which we will explore later in the chapter.

Ideas of progress, knowledge, and intelligence in academic and higher-education culture are challenged by non-Western prepackaged worlds in sayings because they rely on oral history and local knowledge. Refrains and sayings are creative and malleable, though—I argue—they provide certainty and rely on a degree of authority that do not require formal institutional validation. In the Dominican Republic, wisdom and experience undergird how one understands a refrain's root and structure.[5] The message is not without fault; these sayings can at the same time encapsulate biased and prejudiced cultural ideologies, especially in relation to sexism and racism, among other forms of discrimination. Nonetheless, the function of the saying and who gets to tradition it as well as shape it challenge the boundaries of access and knowledge, making learning more accessible and porous. The memorization of refrains can operate similarly to how different religious traditions memorize verses of their sacred scriptures. In the Christian scriptures, Phil. 4:13, "I can do

---

2. See Wenceslao Serra Deliz, *El refranero puertorriqueño: Historia e ideología* (Ponce, PR: Centro de Investigaciones Folklóricas de Puerto Rico, Casa Paoli, 2002).
3. Serra Deliz, *El refranero puertorriqueño*, 44.
4. Serra Deliz, *El refranero puertorriqueño*, 47.
5. Serra Deliz, *El refranero puertorriqueño*, 49.

all things in him who strengthens me" (RSV), operates as if it were a popular refrain. It points to a theological truth, enables practices, and is applied to contemporary contexts instead of its original setting.

Sociologists and linguists look at refrains and how they operate in culture, including, in many cases, how they shape and influence activism. For example, some indigenous and grassroots movements speak of their work as the act of *desalambrar,* or removing the barbwire, typically marking private property.[6] *Desalambrar* not only becomes a physical act, in the case of the recovery of land, but it also becomes a practice in detangling laws and ideologies from its colonial embeddedness. Refrains can hold two or more spaces. Though in this chapter I am arguing for the spiritual transcendence and epistemological value of popular sayings, I do not pretend this work or myself to be decolonized but to strive toward anti-colonialism. The act of writing this chapter forces me to wrestle with the field of Western critical theory as well as to translate *sentipensar*[7] into a second language. I can feel the pricks of wire digging through my hands as I type.

FUNCTIONS: *YHLQMDLG*

Del dicho al hecho, hay un gran trecho (from a saying to its practice, there is a long road). I think about refrains "not [as] an origin but a point of departure,"[8] meaning that they are used, repeated, and remembered to the extent that they say something about the present moment. This gap, *trecho,* or road in a refrain is not empty but filled with context and meaning, while at the same time affording a surplus of meaning as it moves. It is understood and operational in context. English studies scholar Celeste Langan notes that "the refrain opens the question of what is *not* repetition, reminding us that the putative power of words is an effect of neither their form nor their content, but of the 'dynamic positioning', the always contingent social power, of speakers."[9] A Marxist read-

6. See Susana E. Matallana-Peláez, "Desalambrando: A Nasa Standpoint for Liberation," *Hypatia* 35, no. 1 (2020): 75–96, https://doi.org/10.1017/hyp.2019.14; also, Liliana Cotto Morales, *Desalambrar,* 2nd ed. (San Juan, PR: Editorial Tal Cual, 2011).

7. *Sentipensar* means to think-feel and is a term used in Latin American philosophy. See Carmen Cariño and Alejandro Montelongo González, "Coloniality of Power and Coloniality of Gender: *Sentipensar* the Struggles of Indigenous Women in Abya Yala from Worlds in Relation," *Hypatia* 37, no. 3 (2022): 544–58.

8. Celeste Langan, "Repetition Run Riot: Refrains, Slogans, and Graffiti," *Wordsworth Circle* 52, no. 2 (2021): 289, https://doi.org/10.1086/713834.

9. Langan, "Repetition Run Riot," 289.

ing of the power of speech positions refrains as tactics for negotiating social power.[10] In other words, *YHLQMDLG*.[11] Refrains and sayings, as they are traditioned, can evoke the past and echo in the present through their repetition. However, their function is not a recovery of history—its origins—but the message in itself, and at the same time it operates in context and can be influenced by history. Its aim is not to relativize knowledge but to make generalizing claims about life, ethics, morals, and even God.

French philosopher Paul Ricoeur critiques the study of signs, semiotics, as reductive to the study and abstraction of meaning and notes that one cannot know the meaning of a sign for the virtue of the sign in itself. One comes to know because they have received direction toward what it stands for—its context. Ricoeur sees the sentence as an irreducible unit of discourse and the installation of meaning because it is there where dialectic is held and not in its reduction of *langue*.[12] He pairs events with discourse, and when discourse is paired with events, the discourse has meaning[13]—again, context. Ricoeur goes on to argue at the end of his work *Interpretation Theory: Discourse and the Surplus of Meaning* for the appropriation of language in "historicity," where he states that what needs to be appropriated is "the power of disclosing a world that constitutes the reference of the text."[14] He is not concerned by the intended meaning of the author. His concern is rather how the text speaks to us today in ways that keep texts alive. Nonetheless, I think it is important to acknowledge the purpose within those layers and the surplus of meaning of any text (verbal or nonverbal), for in unveiling these meanings, one can uncover the systems of oppression and the systematic development of the imaginary that has led us to our present. Also, maybe not every text should be "kept alive," for it may not bring about life, but rather death if we do not critique and highlight its subtexts.

Venezuelan sociologist of religion Otto Maduro warns about the risk of assuming eternal truths and their universal validity. He notes the importance

---

10. Langan, "Repetition Run Riot," 288.

11. *YHLQMDG* (yo hago lo que me da la gana) is the title of Bad Bunny's second album. It spells the initials for "I do whatever I want." The use of the reference in the text points to the arbitrariness of symbols in relationship to meaning. Also, someone familiar with this cultural reference will likely read the initials as a full sentence without interruption. See Celest Langan, "Repetition Run Riot," 306n4.

12. Paul Ricoeur, *Interpretation Theory: Discourse and the Surplus of Meaning* (Fort Worth: Texas Christian University Press, 1976), 21.

13. Ricoeur, *Interpretation Theory*, 12.

14. Ricoeur, *Interpretation Theory*, 43, 92.

of not denying the complexity and complications of life.[15] His concerns stem from the danger of not interrogating ideologies contained in these refrains as well as the assumption of absolutism they convey. Maduro argued for an understanding of language as a dynamic phenomenon that requires participation. He adds, "To actively and collectively participate in the creative re-appropriation of shared language can promote our capacity to know reality anew in the context [of] oppression we seek to change."[16] The seeming lack of ownership or trademark of sayings can give the impression that refrains transcend the boundaries of sociopolitical and economic class. However, this goes back to the dynamic of power in the use of refrains in the context of the speaker and/or signer.

French philosophers Gilles Deleuze and Félix Guattari understand that refrains organize chaos. They are not limited to words or the written form and can be found in nature, movements, and other types of expressions. The philosophers use the word *ritournelle*, which in English is translated to "refrain." In Spanish, a *ritournelle* is a *tintineo*. It means a clink, a jingle, and the repetition of it. Therefore refrains—sayings—rely on memory and continuity more than historicity and formal institutionalization. I make this distinction because I am thinking about sayings that get repeated, but one does not always, if at all, know its origins, which is what I mean by history. Even the sayings that have little relevance in their literal sense are still used to convey meaning. For example, to say you are short of something or that something did not go as planned, people say, "Me fui a caballo y vengo a pie" (I left on a horse and came back on foot). The context is no longer relevant if horses are not the main mode of transportation. One would have to know that it meant that your horse got tired on the way back and you had to leave it behind. Sometimes people only know half a saying and still it conveys the same meaning as if they knew the whole phrase. For example, "En lo que el hacha va y viene, el palo descansa" (In the meantime the axe comes and goes, the tree rests): in Puerto Rico the first part of the refrain is the most known and typically said when one needs or is encouraged to do something else in between tasks. Typically, half the refrain still conveys a full meaning.

In his memoir, Salvadorian writer Javier Zamora illustrates the *ritournelle* (refrain) when his *tía* (aunt) rushes to share some good news and calls him *tontito* (silly). He reflects, "I like it when she calls me that. The words sound

---

15. Otto Maduro, *Maps for a Fiesta: A Latina/o Perspective on Knowledge and the Global Crisis* (New York: Fordham University Press, 2015), 38.
16. Maduro, *Maps for a Fiesta*, 93.

like rain slipping through holes in our roof, falling into tin buckets we place on the floor, so the room won't flood."[17] For Deleuze and Guattari, a refrain is portable, can be repeated, and holds together many heterogeneous elements in its consistency.[18] As the refrain moves it marks a territory. They argue that the "refrain may assume other functions, amorous, professional, or social, liturgical or cosmic: it always carries earth with it; it has a land (sometimes a spiritual land) as its concomitant."[19] What Zamora invokes in his narration is Deleuze and Guattari's theory; the author organizes the sounds, words, and actions in a vivid image through storytelling that many can hear, not only read.

GROUNDING: *EL PIE FORZADO*, "FORCED FOOTING"

Though linguists argue about the categorization and distinction of phrases, idioms, sayings, refrains, and so forth, Serra Deliz understands the most adequate definition of saying is described by Spanish linguist Fernando Lázaro Carreter. Lázaro Carreter says it is "a complete or independent phrase, literal or allegorical, generally, in an elliptical or judgmental form," that "expresses a thought—an experience, teaching, admonition, etc.—as a judgment in which at least two ideas are related."[20] This definition makes me recall the folkloric use of *pie forzado*. A pie forzado is the theme or rule given to the troubadour (poet or lyricist) in advance for their composition of a stanza. The task of a skilled troubadour is to improvise a *décima* (ten-line stanza) while following one rule: staying within the poetic composition of the rhyme and/or theme of their footing (pie fozado). One does not need to be a troubadour to recognize the rhythm and cadences of a *décima*. Sayings and refrains are a culture's pies forzados. They give social parameters that name practices, biases, lessons, and beliefs that are wrapped in stanzas. They serve as mnemonic devices that are preserved and traditioned. Twits, slogans, and catchphrases have similar functions and purposes within marketing and public relations. However, popular

17. Javier Zamora, *Solito: A Memoir* (Toronto: Hogarth, 2022), 7.
18. Gilles Deleuze and Félix Guattari, *A Thousand Plateaus: Capitalism and Schizophrenia*, with a foreword by Brian Massumi, trans. Brian Massumi (Minneapolis: University of Minnesota Press, 1987), 323.
19. Deleuze and Guattari, *Thousand Plateaus*, 312.
20. "Frase completa o independiente, que en sentido literal o alegórico, y por lo general, en forma sentenciosa y elíptica, expresa un pensamiento—hecho de experiencia, enseñanza, admonición, etc.—a manera de juicio en el que se relacionan por lo menos dos ideas." Lázaro Carreter, quoted in Serra Deliz, *El refranero puertorriqueño*, 54.

sayings are not necessarily only tied to an object or an idea, but to a practice. It can describe a thing or a belief, but it mostly shows a predisposition and/or an action. Going back to "En lo que el hacha va y viene, el palo descansa" and "I can do all things in him who strengthens me," one finds they are descriptive, informative, and ideological but are ultimately tied to a practice; the first to rest and multitasking, the second to endurance and action.

A pie forzado also launches a challenge between two troubadours in the same way a saying holds one or more ideas that present a challenge or encouragement. Sayings mark and take territory. Popular Latin American sayings carry the land and beliefs, in part, for generations of Latinx people in the United States as both tradition and inheritance. Though not always explicitly religious, refrains can negotiate moral, ethical, and theological liminal spaces. Hereunder I use five sayings as examples of how they signal these spaces and serve as groundings.

Más vale maña, que fuerza. *"It's better to have grit than strength."*

In *Theologizing en Espanglish*, Carmen Nanko-Fernández asserts that the place of theology-making for Latinx is in *lo cotidiano*, "the daily life." In this theological task of the day-to-day, one moves and varies the lens of interpretation to focus on a more accurate and holistic interpretation.[21] She argues that God-talk (theopoetics) in the Latinx community's vernacular "requires us to read in nuanced ways the contexts and contours of our situated humanity—in relationship. After all, theologies are the humble articulations of the perennially tongue-tied in the presence of mystery."[22] Similarly, Latino theologian Jean-Pierre Ruiz says, "Although theologians take considerable pains to distinguish between 'general' and 'special' revelation, I would argue that revelation is always particular, that divine self-disclosure takes place in the vernacular, even in the complex particularities of countless vernaculars."[23] This disposition, *maña*, of doing theology in a vernacular that at the same time looks at *lo cotidiano* as *the* source of theology challenges and disrupts the social imaginary and academic/proper status quo because it is mediated by popular production. It is the use of strategy over force. As part of a theological conversation, this saying can aid in

21. Carmen Nanko-Fernández, *Theologizing en Espanglish: Context, Community, and Ministry* (Maryknoll, NY: Orbis Books, 2010), 59.
22. Nanko-Fernández, *Theologizing en Espanglish*, 51.
23. Jean-Pierre Ruiz, *Revelation in the Vernacular* (Maryknoll, NY: Orbis Books, 2021), xxvi.

the practice of evangelism, proselytization, and approach to theological differences. It requires strategizing of experience and knowledge before resorting to force. In spaces of high tension, this "mantra" can be useful.

Se dice mucho con poco. *"You say a lot with very little."*

Latinx popular refrains allude to the established consensus relying on an already-established understanding in context. They assume a collective epistemology. Otto Maduro argues that knowledge works as chains of relationships. He claims that "to know is the particular ability to intervene in reality by imagining relationships among elements that emerge from collective and individual experience."[24] Maduro then calls for an "epistemological humility"[25] that allows people to interrogate and be self-aware of the bits of knowledge that shape them, even the ones they consciously reject. The arrogance of knowledge might delude them from seeing how they operate regardless. Another way of looking at this refrain is through Matt. 7:16 (NRSV), "You will know them by their fruits." It alludes to the practice, to what is done, that says whose—in this case Jesus's disciples—they are.

¡Ay Bendito! *"Oh, good God!"*

"¡Ay Bendito sea Dios!" is a Puerto Rican expression. It is rarely said in its totality. One most commonly would say "ay Bendito," "Bendito," or "dito." It can translate to, but not fully capture, "oh, good God!" Folkloric art curator Teodoro Vidal researches the use of sayings and prayers that are used, mostly in rural Puerto Rico, to control nature.[26] He collects artifacts, rituals, and refrains—incantations—that predate Spanish colonization and Christianity. Prayers, *clamores* (cries), and declarations are part of the everyday language. "Ay Bendito" typically signifies empathy, frustration, compassion, or lament, depending on the intonation, though always laden with deep sentiment. It does not have to be, and most often is not, said in a religious context but a deep existential one beyond ecclesial spaces. This is part of the contribution of paying attention to these refrains as they carry sentiment, meaning, and theological knowledge into everyday life without religious or ecclesial mediation.

24. Maduro, *Maps for a Fiesta*, 110.
25. Maduro, *Maps for a Fiesta*, 137.
26. See Teodoro Vidal, *El control de la naturaleza: Mediante la palabra en la tradición puertorriqueña* (San Juan, PR: Ediciones Alba, 2008).

Nadie aprende por cabeza ajena.
"No one learns using someone else's head."

Brazilian educator and theologian Rubem Alves writes about the process of unlearning to open ourselves up to creativity. The wisdom of culture and its traditionating are tied to our ancestors and the authority they exert in our communities. Beginning the lesson of the refrain with "mi abuela decía" (my grandmother used to say) does not adjudicate authorship but bestows authority to the wisdom of the saying. There is a sense of community and collective responsibility in a community's learning and practices that also depend on the individual. For Alves the teacher is someone who teaches from what they know and explores the idea of learning and teaching about what is unknown.[27] They encourage wonder and exploration. Learning happens in a myriad of ways. Autonomy and agency in learning foster creativity and new content. Therefore, the cultivation of knowledge, if the aforementioned saying is true, necessitates intentional community and care for each individual's subjectivity. This approach is helpful, for example, if we look at ministering and pastoring and the pedagogy behind practices of care and counseling.

Hay mucha tela pa' cortar. *"There is a lot of fabric to cut off from."*

Popular sayings are rich cultural productions. They inform embodied practices. The understanding of these iterations happens in one's body as one carries them. I am not suggesting that the qualitative value of a saying and interrogating is good or bad, but they convey a certainty known in the body of culture. The abundance of meaning, all the available fabric, is created when all the diversity in Latinx cultures in the United States collide in an encounter with each other; thus Latinx ought to be understood as a category of convocation and not a homogenizing of people. Another qualifier that begins the refrain's instruction in spaces of diaspora is "En mi país se dice . . ." (it's said in my country). Many times, folks realize that the refrain is not endemic to their country of origin but shared throughout Latin America, adding to the body of global south epistemologies.

Popular sayings also inform academic writing and research. Scholarship does not exist without the populous; it is political. The world of academia curates what happens in culture and society. But popular knowledges, found on

27. See Rubem A. Alves, *The Poet, the Warrior, the Prophet*, new ed. (London: SCM Press, 2002).

the ground and communal-centered oral cultures, challenge the predictability of empirical clarity and are retained as a form of resistance to the dominant culture. Though some can be traced, most of these knowledges have no singular author, no pure site of origination, and no sole history.

Popular sayings can also inform pastoral care and theological education. Religious discourse is fraught with slogans and theological one-liners. Issues of racism, sexism, Christian supersessionism, and ableism are neatly packaged and traditioned; popular refrains can either perpetuate or disrupt the social messages embedded within. For example, the saying "El pudor de la doncella la hace aparecer más bella" (The modesty of the virginal lady makes her look more beautiful) relates and conflates beauty, sexuality, and morality as virtues. Furthermore, the saying "Esto ya se está pasando de castaño a oscuro" (The situation is going from brown to dark) emphasizes colorism as an ideological virtue or lack thereof. However, messages of transformational practices, justice, and care are also generated in this way. For example, the refrain "Lo que no es igual, es ventaja" (That which isn't equal is an advantage) questions matters of equity; "La codicia rompe el saco" (Greed breaks the bag) warns that eventually one loses all excess of accumulation; "Haz bien sin mirar a quién" (Do good without seeing who it is) invites radical compassion and hospitality.

Conclusion

Popular sayings can be a place where people, cultures, worlds of knowledge, and spirituality meet. During one of the lectures for the *Week of Mass Incarceration* at the Vanderbilt University Law School, Sister Helen Prejean's opening remark mentioned how a Latin American saying best explained her work around advocacy against the death penalty. She used "Ojos que no ven, corazón que no siente," which she translated to "what the eyes cannot see, the heart cannot feel."[28] Sister Helen's adoption of this saying to condense the depth of her work and spiritual telos exemplifies and solidifies the arguments of this chapter. She explained how her work is to make the injustices known so people will act in compassion. Theological work is facilitated to us not only by having hermeneutical tools but also by being able to interpret the context that we tradition using proverbs and refrains. Belonging to no one, refrains, in one breath, impart and expand knowledge, admonition, wisdom, and culture.

---

28. Helen Prejean, "Law Students for Social Justice and George Barrett Program Presents: Sister Helen Prejean," *Week against Mass Incarceration* (lecture, Vanderbilt University, Flynn Auditorium, February 27, 2023).

Works Cited

Alves, Rubem A. *The Poet, the Warrior, the Prophet*. New ed. London: SCM Press, 2002.

Cariño, Carmen, and Alejandro Montelongo González. "Coloniality of Power and Coloniality of Gender: *Sentipensar* the Struggles of Indigenous Women in Abya Yala from Worlds in Relation." *Hypatia* 37, no. 3 (2022): 544–58.

Cotto Morales, Liliana. *Desalambrar*. 2nd ed. San Juan, PR: Editorial Tal Cual, 2011.

Deleuze, Gilles, and Félix Guattari. *A Thousand Plateaus: Capitalism and Schizophrenia*. With a foreword by Brian Massumi. Translated by Brian Massumi. Minneapolis: University of Minnesota Press, 1987.

Langan, Celeste. "Repetition Run Riot: Refrains, Slogans, and Graffiti." *Wordsworth Circle* 52, no. 2 (2021): 287–307.

Maduro, Otto. *Maps for a Fiesta: A Latina/o Perspective on Knowledge and the Global Crisis*. New York: Fordham University Press, 2015.

Matallana-Peláez, Susana E. "Desalambrando: A Nasa Standpoint for Liberation." *Hypatia* 35, no. 1 (2020): 75–96.

Nanko-Fernández, Carmen. *Theologizing en Espanglish: Context, Community, and Ministry*. Maryknoll, NY: Orbis Books, 2010.

Prejean, Helen. "LSSJ and George Barrett Program Presents: Sister Helen Prejean." *Week Against Mass Incarceration*. Lecture, Vanderbilt University, Flynn Auditorium, February 27, 2023.

Ricoeur, Paul. *Interpretation Theory: Discourse and the Surplus of Meaning*. Fort Worth: Texas Christian University Press, 1976.

Ruiz, Jean-Pierre. *Revelation in the Vernacular*. Maryknoll, NY: Orbis Books, 2021.

Serra Deliz, Wenceslao. *El refranero puertorriqueño: Historia e ideología*. Ponce, PR: Centro de Investigaciones Folklóricas de Puerto Rico, Casa Paoli, 2002.

Vidal, Teodoro. *El control de la naturaleza: Mediante la palabra en la tradición puertorriqueña*. San Juan, PR: Ediciones Alba, 2008.

Zamora, Javier. *Solito: A Memoir*. Toronto: Hogarth, 2022.

13

We with God

An (A)Systematic Theology in Five Parts

BRIAN BANTUM

PART I—GOD

We were walking through the park the other day and my five-year-old asked me, "Where is God?" I am not sure what sparked his question. A leaf falling from its branch, the wind chimes woken by the wind, the cat that curled its back up and stared at us as we passed.

"Where is God?" he asked again.

I took his cheeks in my hands and told him to look at me. "God is in my face and God is in your face. Look at your hands. God is in your hands. Look at the stick you've been carrying. God is in that stick."

"God is a stick? God is you? God is me?" he asked.

"Well, no," I said. "God is not you and me and the tree exactly." I was beginning to dig a hole for myself already. "God is in all those things because God holds all those things together," I tried to explain. He does not look convinced.

We bent down over a patch of dirt and I scooped up a little pile and said, "The dirt is us. The hands are God." And I squeezed the dirt and pressed it till the oils and sweat of my palms mixed in and then I spit a bit just for good measure, which made my little boy laugh and laugh. That little pile of dirt became a ball. And I kept squeezing and rolling it in my hand to keep it damp. "I am in this ball because part of me is in it, but the dirt isn't the same thing as me. I'm not the same as the dirt. But it has part of me. It stays a ball because I keep giving it something of myself. I keep giving parts of myself because I want it to be. I want it to be because I love it."

He held his hand out to me. "Can I be God now?" he asked.

PART II—HUMANITY

I woke today. And the first thing I saw was clay like me. Well, almost like me. Some curves in different places and some strange dangling bits. It was red brown and rich. The clay was lighter than me. I am dark and smooth like the earth where the sweetest fruits come from.

I was just turning on my side to stretch when this clay tried to name me. "Woman," it said. The name sounded strange to me, but I was not sure what else I would call myself, so I just kept looking and breathing and taking in this world I found myself in.

We are some of the animals here. We all eat. We run. We nuzzle noses and help to clean each other. We are still giving names to all these other animals we meet. I do not know what they call each other; I guess the names are more for us than them.

But the clay I woke up to, our fingers fit. When I looked up at the tree, they seemed to want to help me reach the sweet, orange globes that hang. And I want to help them. Some of the other animals will come and go. But the clay seems to follow me, and I like to follow them. We seem to know each other's sounds and it feels safer when they are around. There is something that hangs in the air when they see me . . . when I see them. I think it is true for all of us earthen things. We do not have a word for it yet, what hangs in the air between us all, above us, in us, but we know it is there. We clung together and walked together and wandered and held each other when we were afraid. I hope we will be less afraid tomorrow when we wake again.

PART III—WE FELL

My eyes were open.

Brian Bantum

The finches circled and squirrels scrabbled around trees.
They seemed only concerned about food or each other.
Were they so different? These little things fled as we walked
through the trees, or they puffed and snarled the same way each
day, as though we had not just passed by that way yesterday.

I do not puff out my chest or run when I am scared.
I do not curl my back like a cat or snarl like a dog.

No, we are not the same.
We are different.
We are not so weak.
I must be more than that.

We are more than that black horse that runs
in the fields beyond the stream or the cow that
does nothing but graze after we milk it in the
morning.

Yes, I feel hunger gnarl my insides when the
berries have withered, but the salmon have not begun to swarm the river.

Yes, I look at her and imagine my hands running
up her thigh and my mouth on the bend
of her neck.

But I am not like those creatures who mount
each other mindlessly?!

Look at that elephant with its loping heft.
I am so small next to her.
Look at the wolf and her pack.
All I can do is hide if it catches my scent.

No! I am not prey.
I will not be prey.
I am not like them.
I am no animal.
I am human.

I am not small.
I am not weak as I seem.
I am not as unknowing as I feel.
I am not as fleeting as strawberry bushes
at the end of summer
as needy as this one I wake with
as that cow.

I name, I am not named.

Let me snap these branches and weave a basket.
I will wind these fibers into something
to cover my weakness, my desire, my waste.

See!

Even the trees serve me. Let me burn them to
make a field.

See!

I will not hunger again

See!

How I lift these stumps, these
enormous rocks!
(Who cares if she gave birth to new life in
groans and sweat and then somehow
nourished them from her own body.)

See!

I killed the creature that hunted us.
I fed us!

(Who cares if she gathered the wood and crushed the herbs and
turned the roots and bone into broth and the berries into glaze

*and turned the meat over in the fire every ten minutes until it had
the feeling of warm fruit in our mouths.)*

See!

I am not like you. I am not like this world.

See?

PART IV—GOD WITH US

Why would you come to Mary if you were not going to receive anything
from her?
What did you see?
What did you want to learn?
To love?

The way she held her mother or sung her sister to sleep?

Or was it the way she shook when soldiers marched in her streets with spears
heavy from the bloodied bellies of her people on their tips?

Did you need to feel her hunger for your people and the pain of their toil that
filled other people's baskets?

> She walked through dusted streets, her life tilted only toward betrothal,
> marriage, and bearing heirs. For so long the coils of men's words hemmed
> her in, slid her mother's knowings into drawers to be used but not seen.

But you saw what she saw.

As promise knit into muscle and bone you said,

"I want to be raised by you. I want you to teach me to pray. I want your life to
be the life I follow with my eyes as the world becomes known to me. I want to
hear the tremor of your voice when we walk among our neighbors who hunger
and thirst. I want to know the world through your life, your humanity."

How can this be? To see Word and love and woman knotted into Mary's son.

She said yes. God kneaded clay into toes and fingers—eyes opening in the warmth of liquid life, beginning and end listening to garbled voices from within skin and bone. The push, push of a heart that said yes to harboring the holy.

Her breath, her sweat, hope becoming flesh and then from the darkened den she emerges, light pouring from within, you, in your priestess's arms. God swaddled in need, seeking her eyes, rooting for your mother's life. As you slept you brought peace to us, in your need, you fed our longing.

You, God enfleshed, are never without us. We are never without you. Let us be like you; let us be like her.

Part V—We with God

She stepped out from the little closet behind the choir loft in black Jordan shorts and her blue soccer camp t-shirt. The stage had been cleared of the tall cross and the pulpit, and where there used to be a floor there was a deep tub and steps that had sandy grips just like her grandma's house. She looked out on the congregation, her mother, her grandmother, her brother on his phone. The organ hummed and the water in the tub shivered as the bass danced with the drums.

She took her first step and the wet warm climbed her toes to her ankles. Afraid she would slip, warm hands grasped hers as she descended into the pool.

Standing there, waist deep in water . . . "I do" and "I will" fell from her mouth, responding to the whispers of the midwife calling her forth.

"I baptize you in the name of . . ." And she let herself be pressed back, she let herself fall, but her weight was not her own as the water crawled up her sides, up her back, her neck. . . . One last breath.

The water soaked through the strands of her black crown. Her eyes closed. Wet and dark met and the new enfolded her.

Water was everywhere. There was no place where it was not, where it did not cling to her and in the dark the words dissolved into murmuring silence. Chaos. Peace. Muffled sounds . . .

Spirit.
Rise.
Welcome.

Pastor pressed her hand into her back, and words rushed in as the water rushed, her face pressing through the membrane into the world of air again.

The two women held each other, and this newly born creature took her first steps out of the womb, her clothes and hair heavy, stepping out into the world again dripping with God and ready to share.

* * *

What does it mean to do theology in this moment? To teach theology? To live a Christian life? I have to confess that these days I am experiencing a profound need for words to describe what we are living and at the same time a perpetual inadequacy of any analysis I attempt to offer. In some ways the world has become just as much a mystery as God—the more I examine and ponder and read, the more uncertain I become. And yet, here is the world. Here is God. Here is my body and my life. We are here.

What do we begin to say in a world where we have to admit our words are only ever glimpses of what is, whether we are speaking of God or ourselves? But maybe that is the point? Maybe this is the beginning of a recognition that, whether we follow Karl Barth and say God with us, or we with God, there is mystery and wonder and uncertainty on both sides.

If we begin with this, perhaps we might also begin to see the possibilities of our words and lives not in the perfection of their analysis or history or diction, but in how our theology sings. How our theology lives and breathes.

To begin to imagine this we must turn to our artists, make room for our theologians to become artists and artists to become our theologians. Yes, there is a necessity for scholarship in the ways our institutions of higher education are built. And there is something that the artists in our midst offer us as well, that might press out past our classrooms and our conferences into the streets.

At stake for me is a question of what could theology gain from writers alongside critics. Here I am adapting a distinction made by Annie Dillard in *Living by Fiction*. She writes, "A work of fiction is indeed interpretive in the special sense that it is, by intention, an object to be interpreted. Unlike the critic, who intends his interpretation to be near the level of a 'final say,' and who does not, at any rate, expect the world to devote much energy to analyzing his interpretation, the fiction writer intends his work to be a primary object. He intends it to be interpreted." She goes on to suggest,

> The writer is certainly interested in the art of fiction, but perhaps less so than the critic is. The critic is interested in the novel; the novelist is interested in his neighbors. Perhaps even more than in his own techniques, then, the writer is interested in knowing the world in order to make real and honest sense of it. He worries the world and probes it; he collects the world and collates it. No part of it is outside his field. [1]

In a moment when no accumulation of the critic's analysis can help us to recognize, much less pursue, a future, I wonder if the possibility is not in what we say, but in how we say it and who we say it with.

When we see, feel, sense the world, in all of its materiality and complexity, when we express it in a way that aims to draw people into the beauty (or gruesomeness) of a moment, perhaps we can imagine new ways of being in the world right now, that we might be able to read the mystical, the wonder, the awe, the love that resides in the everyday.

We cannot explain what is beautiful about life with God solely from the perspective of the critic—as ones who have collated what others have said about God. If our lives with God are beautiful (and I believe they are), we can only share it.

By share I mean to invite people to feel the power and possibility of their lives, to feel the fear, but not be overwhelmed by it . . . to say that somehow our life with God has some meaning. I suppose it is the difference between telling someone how amazing bread is and taking them to your favorite bakery and letting them taste the way the crust tears away and the flesh melts as you close your mouth. It is the difference between reading a recipe and feeling the dough press between your fingers as you knead it.

While so many of us lament and wonder about the future of theological education and the church, I fear we sometimes miss the hunger of young people, of all people in our midst to taste and see.

Of course, this idea of a theology that speaks of God through the materiality of our world is far from an innovation. You see the birds, there was once a man, Jesus picked up some dirt. . . . Our words about God rise up from the dust of our lives together and return again.

What if our theological education was not only about histories or doctrine or historical method or word studies—all endeavors that are critical to understanding that we are part of long and complicated traditions. What if

---

1. Annie Dillard, *Living by Fiction* (New York: Harper & Row, 1982), 150–51.

theological education was also sitting under a tree and thinking about how to describe the leaves as they fall? About understanding how colors mix and layers of shade give an image depth and contrast and movement?

Just like there is a difference between reading a recipe, tasting bread, and baking a loaf, there is something in the practice of creating, of working our hands into clay, of framing an image just right, that also begins to shape how we see one another, how we see the wonder and miraculous all around us.

"We with God"—there is mystery on both sides. What does it look like when theology, our words about God struggle to become bread? Become taste and scent? I wonder if our theology will begin to sound and read differently? And I wonder if we will also find more of ourselves in this work, if we will help our students to bring more of themselves?

But if I believe in what I am saying, I am already in danger of sharing a recipe instead of inviting you to taste. I am bordering on talking about art instead of offering an experience. So what follows is a small piece of what has been in process for me for the last ten years, my own process of struggling with the inadequacy of my theological writing in the face of the beauty and pain I see.

This series of points creates an (a)systematic theology—a way of pointing to the power of theological stories, of how our ideas about God and humanity and sin and Jesus are all stitched together, implicitly and explicitly, in all that we do—and yet the power and effect of these systems are not always captured in our reflection on ontology or epistemology or transcendence. When theology is artifact rather than the process. I wonder what happens when theology is the struggle of the poet bringing her pencil to a blank page or the painter beginning a color study. I wonder what happens when we think the knowledge is in the process and not confined to the product. If it is the process, then perhaps we can begin to see theology in wider and wider terms. We do not need to fret over the dreaded "and" that leads to so much mental gymnastics—body *and* soul, theology *and* art, individual *and* community—as though the words and realities on either side of the "and" are somehow irreconcilable. Art lives in the "and."

What happens when theology joins her? Does theology begin to look a little different?

In these five reflections I want to ask what it might look like, what it might feel like to become immersed in the story, to see ourselves swimming in it, and what happens when we rise from those waters and enter the world again.

WORKS CITED

Dillard, Annie. *Living by Fiction*. New York: Harper & Row, 1982.

Conclusion

Now Theopoetics, in Living Color

LAKISHA R. LOCKHART-RUSCH AND
OLUWATOMISIN OLAYINKA OREDEIN

Lakisha R. Lockhart-Rusch is LLR and Oluwatomisin Olayinka Oredein is OOO.

LLR: It has been as much an honor as it has been a creative and liberating endeavor to edit this book with you. However, many who are reading this book have no idea how it came into being. I remember you sending an email or a Facebook message asking who was interested and I immediately replied, not even knowing what was going to come of it. I knew that I trusted you and trusted the necessity of this work and these voices to be made flesh in the world. Tomi, you were the ignition of this work, and I am so grateful for you and your vision. So, why? Why did you feel this book needed to be written? Why this book and why now?

OOO: In 2018 I was teaching a seminary class on theopoetics and Black art as theologically expressive but could not find a book resource that had majority minoritized voices. I thought it was a mistake, so I kept looking. Upon searching, I could not even find an anthology featuring half or a third minoritized authors. This was odd to me because I was a part of the (then) current iteration of the Arts, Religion, and Culture (ARC) composed of many minoritized voices doing theopoetics in their religious studies work. It was an anomaly to me that this group had voices doing theopoetic work, but the resources affiliated with theology and arts and theopoetics featured predominantly White voices. For me, the next step was a no-brainer: since there were no resources featuring minoritized authors, I would help create the first! (It is the Nigerian woman in me!) Thus, *Theopoetics in Color* was liberated into the world.

One always hopes that in their current moment in time, they would not be the first to do something or bring something into fruition, but a text/resource did not exist and desperately needed to. In 2024 there needs to be resources that show how minoritized voices are thinking about and doing theopoetics within their respective work. It may not look the same as theopoetics traditionally considered, and that is OK! It is even necessary! If God-talk is not expansive and expanding, it is stagnant. And the one thing Christian theology helped root in my understanding of God and God's movement in the world is that it is dynamic, expansive, never still, and not yet discerned in its entirety. This means those of us in theology and religious studies who implore or engage God-talk and the understanding of God must lend our voices to the ongoing chorus and dialogue parsing out, as best and as contextually as we can, what God sounds like and what God has done and is doing in creation.

This book needs to exist now because those of us who are in this work have always been around doing our work; it is the rest of the world who is now catching up to how we sound and who we already are.

LLR: I couldn't agree more. The more I was reading the chapters in this book, I was picturing the classes that I would be able to teach them in, and I got so excited to be able to give my students this amazing resource and wealth of knowledge, experience, and theopoetic epistemology stemming from all of our minoritized lived realities.

What folks also might not know is that not only is this book a work of brilliant theopoetic expression, but also liberative pedagogy and practice. One of the things that you and I were very clear about was being intentional. We intentionally wanted to preference the voices of scholars of color. We intentionally wanted to make this writing process more human and liberating for all authors (during a pandemic, no less). We intentionally wanted to care for each other as Black women editors with full lives that experience both growth and loss (may your parents' memories be a blessing) during this process. We wanted to live more fully into a more wholesome theopoetic for everyone involved. We wanted to actually live into an embodied approach to theopoetics by attempting to decolonize the theopoetic discourse not only in the writing but in the very style, form, and doing of this work. Can you say more about what the process was like and why it mattered for us, this project, and the readers?

OOO: This process made me hyperaware about contact or interaction. Oftentimes, the details of the publishing process get overshadowed by the emphasis of the deadline. Usually one is in contact with the publication's organizers when they receive a request and when the due date is looming (or passed!). Contact is at a minimum—and understandably so! Life happens in the midst, around, through, in between, and in spite of publishing deadlines. Project organizers typically do not have time to ask about let alone hear and sit with a contributor processing what life is doing to their voice, how it is impacting how and why they write, study, and reflect.

But you and I, we wanted it. We wanted all of it.

What made this process different was that we wanted to acknowledge that the life part is part of the process of writing theopoetically. Everything that happens to us and matters to us makes its way into the timbre of our writing. For some voices contributing to this anthology, what was happening in their lives dictated what they ultimately wrote about. This means that what a lot of organizers dread, happened: chapter subjects changed! And the process that you and I intentionally curated allowed it to be so. This process welcomed the convergence of life and material, for we were convinced (and, I think right to assume) that life is the main muse of the material!

Theopoetics is not just a topic of study for us but an ontological connecting point between experience and expression. It sits in the middle and in the midst of what we do and how we do it. That is what makes this project different. We wanted life to be a part of the process; we considered what we were all going through and dealing with to be integral to our respective sounds. We welcomed it—sounding different, sounding like we were living through something and living into something at the same time—in the work.

We did not run away from the affective messiness of living (life), but bore into it and asked everyone to draw from that very well. In doing so, thirst is quenched in a way that only the soul knows how to describe.

LLR: One of the things that is still sticking with me from this process and what you just said is that "we did not run away from the affective messiness of living." We did not. We leaned into it. We knew that one of the unique things that only we could bring to this work is all being from minoritized identities. With this reality comes so many layers of oppression, suppression, hurt, blame, shame, silencing, impostor syndrome, and lack of care coupled with the mandate to produce—even in and with hostile environments, situations, and colleagues. We wanted folks to have a soft place to land and share in this process. We wanted our authors to know they were not alone both in their writing and in their experiences. So we would meet (virtually, because of the pandemic). We not only created beloved community groups to read and comment on each other's work, but we would also meet and not only talk about the writing but genuinely check in with each other, for hours. We talked about how we were really doing and what we were really needing in life and this process. We listened and got angry with institutions that wronged one of us. We cried and felt the pain of others. We carved out space to vent, cuss, cackle, and to just be our Black and Brown selves, and that was liberating.

One of the things that I think I am most excited about in this work is our intentionality to keep it authored by only people of color. Originally, we had asked the brilliant Callid Keefe-Perry to write our foreword. Which made sense because of his tireless work with ARC, doing the work of theopoetics, and he was the connecting bridge for many of our relationships. However, once we told him our vision of a work solely authored by people of color, he immediately said "of course" and to let him know what he could do to support and promote. This is what I call an ally. They do not try to take up space when they don't need to, but move out of the way and let others do their thing. It was moments like this in the project, that no one knew about, that to me are theopoetic expressions in themselves, and I often stand in awe.

After all of this, what is leaving you in awe? What is staying with you, Tomi?

OOO: To be honest, I was nervous about our foregoing pace and the typical publishing process for a care-focused model of organizing and developing this book, but I am deeply glad (and grateful to you in suggesting a lot of the process we experimented with and walked through) that we did!

We needed to figure out how in a high-stress environment like academia with high-stress expectations like publication projects, we could foreground humanity and humane, communal-centered approaches.

I hate to admit it, but it was hard! I have never experienced slowing down and focusing on the *people* who are part of a project before. It felt difficult because many of us not only do not know how to care about people who are "working for us," for lack of better phrasing. We are, frankly, averse to anything that does not feed the beast of productivity! But, as you suggested and we often reminded each other, we wanted this to be different. We did not want to feel drained at the end of this, but enlivened. Now *that* is an anomaly: for a publication to invigorate instead of take from us!

This means that our mindsets had to be intentionally (and for me, often) reset! Our colleagues were not producing for our project but for the process. You and I were invested in how each colleague *encountered* their own process! Our focus was counterintuitive to what we scholars typically know how or are trained (maybe even thrown into) to do: attunement to process requires care. We only knew the former model—productivity demanded results. But the only result we wanted was for our colleagues to be true to their voice, prioritize their lives and wellness, and be proud of their work. We wanted to give instead of take away from them; and the best way to do that was to practice care—in check ins, in deadline extensions, in softness, in being real with one another, and in everything else that we do not typically associate with creating a work.

In experimenting with this process, I think we started to do something that allowed the act of creating to be enveloped in something like love for self and care for one another. It showed me that there are different ways to be and exist in academia, and this is when the book had not even been published yet! If academia can learn to be a fraction of this, I think it would be a more enjoyable place. The terminology of "possibilities" is used often in academia, but this was the first real glance that *I* have received about being and living differently into what we do by caring for who we are.

llr: Yes, and I hope that our writers feel the same. I hope that our authors felt cared for, heard, understood, supported, and human. Which, as scholars of color, we do not often feel in the academy. I hope they remember how it felt to not just to push to produce but to listen to their own voices and prioritize their mental, physical, and spiritual needs. I think it is this care that made this work so personal and dynamic.

ooo: I hope everyone prioritizes wellness as part of their creative/constructive process, not as a private act but as a public practice. I think making it public invites a subversive kind of accountability—less pressure filled, and more reflective, slower, soft.

I hope that as we all organize and lead future projects that we embed what we want and find most important into the process—care, recognition, attentiveness to one another and dynamics of production in the modern academy—so that the project leaves a lasting impression. Sure, the content is important, but it is not the most important thing. The people are.

How can our colleagues remember, through their practices, that people are the most important thing?

LLR: How can you as the reader remember to also care for yourself? How can you not put the product over the people or yourself? What might you need to shift, rethink, innovate, be more creative about that makes more space for the humanity and dignity of all persons involved? What mindsets might need to shift?

I hope if you leave with nothing else from this book, that you leave knowing that it can be done differently and that it is equally important, intellectual, and necessary in the academy and the world. The theopoetic expressions in this book are ontological realities that are indeed epistemological pathways. Ways of knowing and making meaning of the style, shape, form, and very movement of life and theology.

OOO: I want people who read this book to wonder about processes of creation instead of worrying about processes of production. I want them to see this book as permission to reimagine what scholars of religion do contentwise and methodologically. Perhaps they can imagine liberationist values to be (a means of) methodology in itself. I want them to see evidence of how care signals not only a kind of moral value system but, most urgently, a serious scholastic approach.

I want readers and engagers of this work alike to realize that religious scholarship is dynamic and fluid, thus values such as communal care are means of expanding notions of "rigor" and "scholarship" often trapped into White-cishetero-male voice and epistemology. There is more than one way to be; thus, there is more than one way to think, speak, analyze, and make connections.

Those of us in *Theopoetics in Color* are doing the work of showing the world where and how the dialogue has expanded, where it has already been happening in theological and religious frameworks that look for total freedom. I call this work liberationist because it aims to demonstrate a different way of being, a framework of "another."

LLR: As we think about this liberationist work that we both cannot wait to be made flesh, to hold in our hands, and to provide as a resource for our students and colleagues, what is your greatest hope for theopoetics in the future?

OOO: I hope theopoetics continues in whatever manner it so chooses. I think it is a lost opportunity if we restrict it and think it only relevant in some scholastic circles. Though this book invites minoritized scholars to explore and do theopoetics, I would be remiss to think it is only happening in academic venues. Theopoetics is bigger than that, more practical than sometimes scholarship around it would have us believe.

This, of course, invites risk: we in academia cannot place a coveted bubble around theopoetics and call it our own discipline or area of expertise. We have to let it be all it is: practical, evolving, in motion, hard to contain. But our academic instincts may bristle at this since we are trained early on to know "what to call ourselves" based on what we have studied and subsequently "mastered."

Theopoetics in its fullness, a fullness we all are still trying to grasp, is not interested in the boundedness of rigid categories. It can exist in categories, but most certainly has always lived outside of them. If one reads Rubem Alves for example, one gets a sampling of how wide the range of theopoetics can be. And *Theopoetics in Color* invites its engagers to not be afraid of range, but to wonder openly and imaginatively and collectively about it. Theopoetics being itself is a wonder. That it invites all who engage with it to do the same is a gift.

LLR: Amen and Ase.

Acknowledgments

"Thank you" cannot express the gratitude and love we feel for our families, friends, peoples, communities, students, peers, colleagues, and cheerleaders. Everything we share in this world is for and about our people; they are us and we are them. As long as we are here, they are, too. And together, we proudly embody the fullness of all we are.

Contributors

BRIAN BANTUM is Neal F. and Ila A. Fisher Professor of Theology at Garrett-Evangelical Theological Seminary, writing and teaching at the intersections of identity, anthropology, and the arts.

CLÁUDIO CARVALHAES is a Brazilian earth thinker, theologian, liturgist, performer, artist, and professor of worship at Union Theological Seminary in New York City.

JOYCE DEL ROSARIO is a Filipina American scholar, writer, and community gatherer based in Seattle, Washington.

YARA GONZÁLEZ-JUSTINIANO is a Puerto Rican author, scholar, and cook and assistant professor of religion, psychology, and culture with emphasis in Latinx studies at Vanderbilt University.

JAMES HOWARD HILL JR. is a writer, photographer, and scholar who teaches and conducts research pertaining to the Black study of religion at Boston University.

CAROLINA HINOJOSA-CISNEROS is a Tejana, Chicana, and *mujerista* artist and scholar and doctoral student in English at the University of Texas at San Antonio.

Contributors

YOHANA AGRA JUNKER is a Brazilian educator, visual artist, and facilitator who teaches art, religion, and culture at Claremont School of Theology.

PEACE PYUNGHWA LEE is a Korean diasporic writer, translator, interfaith spiritual director, and tarot reader who is passionate about living into the beauty and wisdom of her ancestral spiritual traditions.

LAKISHA R. LOCKHART-RUSCH is a womanist play facilitator and innovative educator who teaches at Union Presbyterian Seminary in the area of Christian education.

OLUWATOMISIN OLAYINKA OREDEIN is a Nigerian American creative and scholastic writer who teaches in the areas of constructive theology and ethics and Black religious traditions at Brite Divinity School.

PATRICK B. REYES is a Chicano elder, bestselling author, child futurist, and dean of Auburn Theological Seminary.

TIFFANY U. TRENT is a theatre director and teacher who chairs the department of theatre and drama at the University of Michigan and studies theatre for youth, applied theatre, and practical theology.

TAMISHA A. TYLER is a theopoet, scholar, and artist who serves as a visiting assistant professor of theology and culture and theopoetics at Bethany Theological Seminary.

LIS VALLE-RUIZ is a Puerto Rican playful decolonial scholARTivist who teaches worship and preaching and directs the community worship life at McCormick Theological Seminary in Chicago, Illinois.

Index